CHEWABLES:

40 Days
to an Overall
Healthier YOU

CALEB ANDERSON

Chewables
© 2010 Caleb Anderson

Special thanks to
The YMCA of Pierce and Kitsap Counties
1614 S. Mildred Street, #1
Tacoma, WA 98465
http://ymcapkc.org

Editorial: Arlyn Lawrence
Design: Brianna Showalter
Book Packaging: Scribe Book Company

Printed and bound in the United States of America by Color House Graphics, Grand Rapids , MI

ISBN: 978-1-4507-3748-7
To order: http://CalebAnderson.net/chewables

calebanderson.net/Chewables
facebook.com/Chewables.ca

This copy of CHEWABLES belongs to

_____

Given by:_____Date:_____

STARTING OUT

"The first wealth is health." – Ralph Waldo Emerson

You are more than just a body. "Health" means more than just not being sick. Fundamentally, health is about the well-being of your whole self—everything that makes up you—including:

- physical attributes
- mental capacities
- emotional engagement
- spiritual awareness

All of these things weave together and act as one, making you who you are and giving you your current experience of life as you know it. That's how you were designed.

A common misconception about health is that it's primarily about physical disease, weight, or exercise. It's much more than that. In fact, Webster's Dictionary defines **health** as "a flourishing condition: well-being."

Are **you** enjoying a state of well-being?

Do you feel like you're **flourishing**?

If you're like me—and like most people—you might feel as though some areas of your life are "flourishing" while others are stagnant or unhealthy. That's because human beings are highly complex creatures. There is more to you than meets the eye. You have a body. You have a mind. You have emotions. And you have a spirit.

The spiritual awareness part of you—while invisible—suggests to your consciousness that there is more to life than what you see and touch. It reminds you that you have a Maker who has had your unique design in mind all along. Not only that, but He's given you a reason and a purpose to live.

Your emotional faculties manage your feelings, personal relationships, and interactions with others and with your own self-image. Emotions at their best invigorate and enhance your life. When they are damaged or out of control, they can work to your detriment. That's why emotional self-care is an important part of holistic health.

Your mental capacities make sense of the world around you. Your mind is always engaged—the left brain analyzes and calculates; the right brain senses and reacts. Your body does what your mind tells it to do. Your emotional and spiritual well-being, as well, are very much influenced by what your mind chooses to focus on, and the meaning it assigns to incoming data.

Physical well-being is the most obvious of all because it's visible and tangible—and most people are visually oriented. That's one reason people are so concerned about the health and appearance of their bodies. And, after all, this body is the only one you get. There's no new model or replacement if you're not careful with the one you were given.

Because of the complexity with which humans were designed, the health of our physical bodies will only be sustained by the health of our whole person—by our overall well-being. That's what this book is about.

In it, I hope to give you simple, impactful encouragement about how to increase or maintain the health of all four aspects of who you are: body, mind, heart, and spirit.

I have no idea where this book finds you. You might be bored and simply flipping through random pages. You might have a twinge of guilt about a particular pattern in your life you know is unhealthy. Or, you might be desperate for change, knowing that if it doesn't happen, severe consequences are right around the corner.

Wherever you find yourself, I hope this little book will be a significant tool on your journey toward health. Like a good multi-vitamin, taken daily and over time, the principles and ideas in this book can contribute to your overall health and well-being.

Life's journey is unpredictable. You never know what tomorrow has in store. But you can choose now to be prepared to make the most of whatever comes. Expect great things, but make good of anything. Prepare today by building healthy habits that lead toward comprehensive, lifelong well-being and health.

Consider inviting someone else to join you along the way. It may be a spouse or significant other. It could be a small group from church, a friend from the Y, a neighbor, or a friend. Most would agree that we need other people on this journey of life...that life is enriched as one person's story intersects or touches another's.

These 40 daily readings were written to be accessible to a wide spectrum of people—young adults, older adults, professionals, students, people who enjoy exercise, people who don't, people with faith convictions, and people who've never set foot in church. It is my hope that no matter what your background, you will find within these pages hope and inspiration as you become a healthier version of YOU.

I'm glad to be with you on the journey. Enjoy!

YOUR CHEWABLES MENU

In the same way that vitamins target and strengthen certain areas of the human body and function, each of the 40 daily readings in this book will enrich a particular component of YOU. As you work through them, look for these icons that will identify how the ideas and concepts in that day's reading will relate to specific areas of your life:

 BODY Your body will build if you make it or break down if you let it. We need regular reminders to protect and care for our physical selves. *Chewables* will help you consider simple yet meaningful ways to maximize the body you've been given.

 MIND Your mind is the most powerful tool you have. But it's also the most difficult to manage. *Chewables* will challenge your thinking, and encourage you to renew your mind and enjoy a life of health.

 HEART Your emotions dictate your life more than you likely realize. When your "heart" (the seat of your emotions) is healthy, your reasoning is clearer, your reactions are more controlled, and your relationships will flourish.

 SPIRIT You are a spiritual being before you are anything else. *Chewables* reminds you of that reality, and challenges you to consider what you're doing to promote your own spiritual health and growth.

 EXTRA SUPPLEMENT At the end of each reading, you'll find opportunities for self-reflection and practical application. Take advantage of them. They are like extra nutritional supplements over and above your daily vitamins!

12

 body
HUMAN MOVEMENT

1

"The great thing in the world is not so much where we stand, as in what direction we are moving." – Oliver Wendell Holmes

I know a guy named Bob who refuses to exercise. He pretends to take pride in the fact that he hasn't worked out in over 20 years. He says, "Exercise for me is getting in and out of my car."

Bob hasn't always been out of shape. In high school he was a great athlete, letterman's jacket and all. But early in his twenties, he was in a motorcycle accident and sat for months in multiple casts. With rods and screws in his bones, his exercise was limited for a year. He gained 30 pounds and stopped caring about his physical health.

"Now," he says, "there's no going back."

It's difficult for any athlete who once performed at a high level to continue to play his or her sport as athletic skills begin to noticeably deteriorate. Here's a news flash (if you didn't already know): all of us are deteriorating physically until we ultimately die. That's the human reality.

But we don't have to speed the process.

Physical movement helps prevent—or at least minimizes—deterioration. But when we stop moving we start losing. Here are the basic elements of all human movements:

- Standing and locomotion (moving from one place to another)
- Raising and lowering center of mass
- Pushing and pulling
- Rotation

Exercise is simply adding resistance, force, and/or speed to the basic human movements. Simple, right? And potentially encouraging. Most human beings who have not been paralyzed can do something, if not everything, on the list of movements. That means we can exercise.

Physical exercise can be intimidating for some and seem like a hopeless endeavor for others. But that doesn't have to be the case any more. If you sit and then stand up, that combines two of the basic human movements and is the foundation for exercise. All you have to do now is begin to think about slightly increasing your intensity level over time. If you like this train of thought, then stay with me. Fight the tendency to associate exercise with marathons and heavy weights. Maybe you'll get there one day, but it doesn't matter.

Think simple movements.

Set simple goals.

Make steady progress.

Make it a point to celebrate small victories. If you want to see physical change in your life, it will happen as you begin to incorporate small steps into regular routines.

Question: What aspects of exercise have been most challenging for you (i.e. inconsistency, not seeing desired or tangible results, intimidation, discouragement, etc.)?

Action: Set a tiny goal right now. Not "I want to lose 100 pounds," but rather a small goal that you can reach within a week. When you reach that goal, celebrate (in a healthy way)! And then set another small goal for the following week.

_____

_____

_____

_____

_____

_____

_____

_____

_____

_____

"Baby step onto the elevator...baby step into the elevator...I'm in the elevator!" – Bob Wiley, *What about Bob?*

spirit
SPIRIT GOGGLES

2

"The latest research shows that spirituality has remarkable healing powers, whether or not you're a member of an organized religion."
– *Self* magazine, September 2007

One of the first activities I ever coordinated for the Y was hosting a "speed dating" event. I'd never participated in speed dating myself, nor did I know anything about hosting an event. I'd only seen it in movies. Just thinking about the whole idea and everything that could go awry made me sweat.

The event came together in a few short weeks. It was simple, but people came. There is even one couple still together today as a result—a genuine Y "love connection."

The morning before the event I received a phone call. There was a young man on the other end of the phone with a question about speed dating. I asked what I could do for him. After stuttering for a bit, he asked about the nature of the gathering. I assured him it would be safe and informal. He pressed for more information, asking specifically about the "type" of people I expected. I was a little nervous about the direction the call was headed, so I assured him of the friendly and conservative atmosphere and tried to end the call. But then he got honest with me.

"Here's the thing," the young man started nervously. "I'm not a good-looking man. And I guess I just wanted to know if it's worth coming or if I will feel embarrassed and overlooked."

My heart broke. What could I say? How could a few kind words make a difference when this young man has been beaten up by his "unattractiveness" his whole life—in this culture where (physical) looks are seemingly everything?

I don't remember what I said, but I tried to encourage him. I tried to assure him that he is much more than just a physical body. I looked for him that night. He didn't come.

Whether or not you're insecure about your physical body, I want to tell you a similar thing today: You are more than meets the eye.

In fact, you're a spiritual being: "So God created people in his own image; God patterned them after himself; male and female He created them" (Genesis 1:27). We are not, and will never be, gods. But, like Himself, God made us spiritual. And our spirits will live on past our physical lives.

Unlike physical bodies, which get old, break down, and eventually give up, our spirits are designed to do the opposite. They can infinitely grow and get stronger. "So we do not give up. Our physical body is becoming older and weaker, but our spirit inside us is made new every day" (2 Corinthians 4:16).

We need spirit-goggles. That's like beer-goggles, but not.

What if you could see past the thin layer of the physical today and into a spiritual reality? What if we saw people as eternal, spiritual beings, created in God's image – instead of as fat, skinny, pretty, tall, etc.?

Life is more than what we see with our eyes. There is a spiritual realm that is as real as what we know as "real life." And I think something inside of you knows it's true.

If you have not seriously considered these possibilities before, I encourage you to start. In many ways, your "spiritual health" is the most important health of all.

 "We are not human beings having a spiritual experience. We are spiritual beings having a human experience." – Teilhard De Chardin

List activities that you associate with increasing your spiritual health. Are you giving an adequate amount of time to them?

_____

_____

_____

_____

_____

_____

_____

What impact do you think your spiritual health has on the rest of your life? _____

_____

_____

_____

_____

_____

_____

mind
SCRIPTING CHANGE

3

"Progress is a nice word. But change is its motivator and change has its enemies." — Robert Kennedy

Did you know that the offensive coach almost always scripts the first 10 to 15 plays of any professional football game? Before the offense ever sets foot on the field, before they look across at the defense, and before they even determine where their starting position will be, they have scripted their first moves.

The scripted plays are based on what the teams know about their opponents and what they know about themselves. If a team has a young quarterback and wants to ease him into the game to let him get comfortable before having to make a big play, the offensive coach will script run plays to start the game. If the coach has great confidence in the quarterback and wants to shock the defense and jump out to a fast lead, he'll likely script them to start throwing the ball aggressively. Either way, these kinds of decisions are made in practice well before the game starts.

In their book *Switch*, Dan and Chip Heath talk about learning to "script" specific changes you want to see in your life, organization, or community. They argue that it's not enough to make vague, blanket statements about changes you hope to see. "I want to eat healthier," is not clear enough. There's wiggle room, space for the rationalizer in all of us. Instead, more appropriate scripting would be "No more white flour, no more whole milk, and no eating past 8:00 p.m."

My brother Josh went to several doctors about some digestive trouble he was having. One doctor just gave him a pill and said he'd likely deal with this issue the rest of his life—basically said, "good luck." Josh wasn't satisfied, so he got another opinion. The new doctor did some preliminary examinations and then gave Josh a major challenge. "I think you're allergic to gluten. If you want to be sure, and if you want your stomach to heal, you need to completely cut the following out of your diet: grains, flour, breads, pastas ... anything with gluten ingredients."

Tough decision. Limit your diet to 25% of the grocery store, or continue with a lifestyle of digestive pain. But the decision was clear—it was black and white. There was no guesswork. Josh took the challenge, and he's a more fit, healthy, and happy man for it.

 Think about the opening quote to today's reading: "Progress is a nice word. But change is its motivator and change has its enemies."

Is there an area in your life where you would like to see progress, but you haven't yet been clear about what "success" would look like? Use this space to jot down some of your thoughts about what those desired successes might be. Then think about what specific changes you need to "script" into your life, in advance, in order to make progress and accomplish your goals.

Example:

Problem: I'm not drinking enough water.
Scripting the Solution: I'm going to keep a glass on my desk all day. When it's empty, I get up and fill it.

Notice the difference between an observation that change is needed (I need to drink more water), and a scripted plan for how, practically, the change can occur (I'm going to keep a glass on my desk all day. When it's empty, I get up and fill it).

Yes, it's simple. The most important principles in life are simple. The hard part is putting them into practice...like, right now.

_____

_____

_____

_____

_____

_____

_____

_____

_____

_____

_____

_____

_____

heart
THE NEW GIFT

"We cannot do great things. We can only do little things with great love." – Mother Teresa

Are you a cop-out gifter? Do you buy presents the same day you have to give them, forcing you to overpay and settle for limited options? In those situations, I invariably end up guessing at what may or may not be relevant to the person's life, activities, or desires. And (honestly), I'm protecting myself from being emotionally vulnerable.

"I'll just get him something basic, something non-risky. He may not want or need it, but it's a typical gift. This kind of gift is expected, normal, easy. Anything affectionate or creative would be presumptuous—like he'd care, or cheesy—as if I could pull it off."

The average gift-giver spends about $30 on a gift for a significant other, close friend, or family member. And my personal conclusion is that, most of the time, it's a wasted $30.

Did you know that over 60% of the money we spend on gift cards goes unused? That's a great statistic for any business that sells gift cards. But it's a dangerous gift for a sensible gift-giver. I have four gift cards in my drawer right now (and I've probably lost four others). They are months if not years old. I don't want to carry them around with me in my wallet. And I rarely make intentional trips to specific stores for the purpose of spending $25 on my card. Not to mention, you never spend just $25—another reason why retailers love gift cards. And rarely will a store give you the remaining value on card back in cash, so you almost have to spend it all, which ends up being more like $35 or $40. So now, the gift your brother got you has cost you money. And all you got was a book you might not like or a DVD you might never watch.

Gift-giving needs to change. I know our economy is hurting. But it should be. In America, we've spent like idiots for decades. Much of what we buy for ourselves we don't need. Thus, almost everything bought for us by others is just clutter on top of existing chaos. Let's stop the madness.

My Grandma Patricia (Pat) turns 80 years old today as I'm writing this. That's a big one. Uncle Jack is buying her an iPad. Okay, I admit, that's a cool gift. And she'll use it. (Grandma Pat's on Facebook, too, by the way.) But my wife and I have been brainstorming for days what we can afford to get Grandma Pat, and nothing of real value has come to mind. She and Grandpa Jake have way more money than we do. They wouldn't want us to spend our limited resources on something they could've bought for themselves if they really wanted it. So we decided to write a poem.

Here's why poems, letters (not cards because they aren't really your words), and other personal gifts are the best:

- They require thought
- They show that you actually know and care deeply for the person
- They don't take up much space in someone's home
- They usually describe a person's good qualities and what you appreciate about them
- It's a healthy emotional exercise – especially for guys
- Electronics and sweaters rarely produce tears

Now I admit, it's different if you're shopping for a child. But if the person is over 16 and you can't afford an over-the-top present, here are the new gifts—which are actually the oldest gifts—you can give forever without regret:

23

1. Create or write something meaningful, or
2. G.C.D. – Give Cash, Dummy

"I can live for two months on a good compliment." – Mark Twain

Question: When was the last time you expressed your genuine love to a family member or close friend?

_____

_____

_____

_____

_____

_____

_____

_____

_____

_____

Action: Take a risk right now. Write a letter to someone close to you. Tell him or her what he (or she) means to you. Describe what you appreciate most about him/her. Don't send it as an email. If you can, give it as a gift, in person. Otherwise, "snail-mail" it, signed by hand. Do it. It's good for your heart. It's good for your health.

mind
ME, TOO

There was as boy named Tommy—probably 16—who sat in a YMCA by himself one day. Tommy had been in a dirt bike accident that resulted in the amputation of most of his left leg. His parents made him go to the Y twice a week after school, just like he used to do. But now Tommy hated it. He could not do the activities he once did. He felt like everyone looked at him and felt sorry for him. So he sat alone.

A cycling class let out and the members walked from the room towards the exit. A man coming out of the class walked with a quick pace and a seemingly normal stride. Tommy didn't see the man approaching, but the man saw Tommy.

"Hi. I'm Dave," the man offered.

"Hi," was all Tommy responded.

"When was your accident?" Dave asked Tommy.

"It's been eight months."

"Do you work out while you're here?" Dave asked, pressing Tommy's comfort level.

"No... not much motivation any more. And, obviously, I'm limited," Tommy said, making eye contact with Dave for the first time and motioning toward his legs.

"I get it," Dave said. Then he lifted the right leg of his sweat pants, revealing an aluminum rod.

"It's been eight years for me," Dave continued. "It gets easier. I promise. How about you and I work out together next time?"

Not only did Tommy's countenance change, his whole perspective changed in that moment. He wasn't alone.

Do you know why support groups like AA, Celebrate Recovery, or Journey To Freedom are successful? Sure, the material is good. But do you know why it really works, essentially? Because we all need to know we're not alone.

1. There is a Creator-God ("Higher Power") who actually cares and is mysteriously involved in our lives.
2. There are other people who can relate to our situation, empathize with our pain, and encourage us to keep on going.

As human beings, there are really no new issues. Everything is common on some level.

None of us are alone. And it's our privilege as Y staff to make sure all our members are keenly aware of this reality.

Writer Anne Lamott says that the most powerful sermon in the world is just two words: "Me, too."

How did today's reading speak to you? Is there a sense you have about someone you need to reach out to? Are you the one who needs to connect with others; do you need to find support in some area of your life? Where will you start?

_____

_____

_____

_____

_____

body
PREHAB

"Life is but a mass of habits—practical, emotional, and intellectual... systematically organized for our greatness or grief." – William James

You've heard of "rehab" – or rehabilitation. It's a place we go when an injury, addiction, or depression digs a hole for us and we need help to get out. Think, for example, of a famous football player who begins his season with such excitement and optimism about the year, only to step into a diving defender during the first quarter of the first game, tearing his knee in several places. That player is finished for the season. In fact, he'll spend the entire year in rehab trying to build his knee back to the state it was in before the hit.

Prehab is the opposite. Where rehab is after the fact—getting us back to where we were—prehab is preventative and progressive. Prehab is about building strength and health so that you don't need rehab.

When you're prehabbing you're preparing. You're anticipating challenges ahead. You're getting yourself—and keeping yourself—in a posture to maintain health and overcome obstacles.

Prehab leads to sustainability.

I've heard a lot of people say that they would get into shape if they had a goal or event or contract (like a professional athlete) to drive them. I think that's a cop-out. That's like saying you won't ever pray because you're not a professional minister. Or you won't process your feelings because you're not a paid counselor. That's being short-sighted.

We all have the capacity to build habits into our lives to sustain health. And while short-term goals are good tools, we can't use the excuse that there's nothing to motivate us. Really, it's longevity of health, happiness, and effectiveness that should drive us, don't you agree?

If nothing's motivating you toward health and fitness these days, it's time for you to develop a new motivation. Try these affirmations to get you going:

1. Physically, I want to have more energy, wake up alert, and exercise four days a week.
2. Mentally, I want to identify my negative thoughts and intentionally replace them with empowering truths, morning and night.
3. Emotionally, I want to train myself to forgive quickly and maintain a confident posture in every new situation.
4. Spiritually, I want to pray a prayer of gratitude and look for someone else I can serve every day.

None of those habits will put you on the fast track to fame and fortune. But that's for the better. The habits above will begin to build sustaining health and happiness into your life. And that's the kind of fortune that pays the best and biggest dividends.

As you make your way through this book, build your own list of healthy habits that work for you. There is no special formula you have to follow. You know you. I'm just reminding you about truths and ideas we all tend to forget and lose sight of in the chaos of life.

Happy prehabbing...

 Choose one of the four affirmations above—or write your own—and focus on it this week. Write it down; tape it to your mirror. Convince yourself that it's really what you want and then take steps toward it.

_____

_____

_____

_____

heart

WINNING AS PLAY

My friend Cliff is a legendary volleyball personality in the greater Seattle area. He is 55 years old and still the ringleader of the small sub-culture of men's beach volleyball players in the area. Twenty years ago, he was one of the best players, winning most of the tournaments he entered. At 55, he's still tough to beat.

There are a couple of secrets to Cliff's lasting success in the Northwest beach volleyball scene.

1. He's never stopped playing. He's never taken more than a month off at a time. And he plays three or four days a week. He went so far as to build a state-of-the-art sand court in his front yard. I'm willing to drive an hour both ways just to play at Cliff's.

There's a lot to be said for simply being consistent. Even if you don't have the natural physical abilities of others, if you refuse to give up, you'll eventually get to a satisfying place.

2. Cliff treats volleyball as play. Even though he is a great player, and has had tremendous success, it's still just a game for Cliff. He doesn't take himself or the sport too seriously.

Now don't get me wrong. Every single game Cliff plays—even at 55 years old—he tries to win. But win or lose, he plays because he enjoys it.

I think many parents and coaches have taken the "fun" out of sports for too many kids. Without realizing it, they are shaping kids' futures— not only in sports, but in many aspect of competitive life.

My college coach almost ruined volleyball for me. I didn't play the sport for two years after finishing with his team. Why? It wasn't fun anymore. I was playing at the Division One level, but I wasn't satisfied because I wasn't enjoying it. Our coach made me and my teammates feel like we weren't good enough, regardless of the effort we put in day in and day out.

Sports are supposed to be games. And games are meant to be enjoyed. The team that finishes the game with the most points wins... that game. But there is always another game to be played. And there are an infinite number of contributors to the outcome:

- Past performance and training
- Emotional state, life events
- Practice time and effort
- Health
- Team performance and effort
- Team chemistry
- Weather conditions
- Officiating
- Match-ups with the opponent
- And list goes on...

Some players and coaches are paid a lot of money to anticipate, align, and generally manage the above factors. But for the vast majority of us, sports are games to be enjoyed. And they are meant to teach us about ourselves and other aspects of life.

Yesterday I was at Cliff's house playing beach volleyball. He and I were teammates. We were playing well and beating a younger team. It was a beautiful day, and Cliff even had cold drinks for us after the games. Hard not to enjoy.

Cliff asked me if I'd be playing in the upcoming tournament. I told him I didn't think I wanted to travel and make the effort because I hadn't won any tournaments this summer thus far. Without a quality partner, I had no chance of winning this one.

"You know," Cliff responded, "if there was a switch, like a light switch, and I could flick it one way and win every single tournament, never losing.... or, I could flick it the other way, never win a tournament, but always have fun playing volleyball, I'd take having fun, no question. It's not worth winning if you're wound so tight you can't enjoy it. I try to just live in the moment."

The ironic thing is, Cliff wins... a lot.

It seems I need regular reminders like this one not to take myself too seriously. Life is short. I want to enjoy it. I'm sure you do, too. When we focus on living in the moment—in the here and now—our attention to detail, our intensity, and even our performance will improve. It's when we start looking to the scoreboard and worrying about outcomes that we forget to focus on the little things that win games.

Question: In what ways are you too worried about outcomes and not enjoying the journey?

_____

_____

_____

_____

_____

_____

_____

Action: Play a game today, just for fun. Win or lose, make sure you don't take it—or yourself—too seriously.

THE WORLD'S GREATEST EXERCISE

"We cannot do everything at once, but we can do something at once." – Calvin Coolidge

There's an older gentleman named Joe who works out at my local Y. At first glance, you wouldn't think of him as an avid exerciser. He's heavy. He wears stabilizing shoes. And his workout apparel is not the latest and greatest from Under Armour® or Lulu®.

And yet, there he is. Five days a week, like clockwork.

He's only on the main floor with equipment for about 10 minutes. Then he does this walk-swim motion in the pool before sitting in the sauna. That's his routine, and he's faithful to it.

When asked about his 10-minute lifting sessions Joe said, "Well, I know it's not much. But, to tell you the truth, I started at about 10 seconds. So I feel pretty good about where I am today." He made himself laugh. "I really like doing pull-downs—the exercise on a cable where you pull the bar from overhead to your chest, I guess mainly because no part of my body hurts when I do it," he added with another chuckle. "I just do a couple exercises that I like to do, and I figure I'll add more the stronger and more confident I get."

Genius.

Joe has discovered the World's Greatest Exercise. Do you know what it is? The World's Greatest Exercise is...the one you'll do.

Seriously.

A lot of people have great intentions for their workouts. They have lofty goals. Or they recall the physical stamina they once had in their youth and use that as their standard. *Chewables* has a message for that person: Lower the bar.

Here's the ironic thing: When you lower the bar that's preventing you from taking action, you actually raise your standards. Right now, the higher bar—be it comparing yourself to others or to the college-aged version of you, etc.—is preventing you from having any real standard in the present. You might think you have high standards, but it's very likely just a façade that's keeping you from action.

By taking a small step immediately, like Joe is doing, you break the pattern of being defeated. Whether you're experiencing a workout slump, a rut, or a long vacation from exercise, you can jump back in and spare yourself the guilt of not being where you think you ought to be. Where you think you should be is an illusion. You are where you are, and you can only start there.

Furthermore, you can reject comparisons. It's counter-productive to compare yourself to others. The person who compares is the only person who cares. No one else cares. Those other people are just focused on themselves anyway. You have to focus on you. Only you can take your next step.

Lower the bar and raise your current standards.

 Question: What are some mental images or ideals you have for your body (or for your fitness routines) that are preventing you from taking immediate action? _____

_____

_____

_____

_____

_____

_____

What is a simple, attainable next step you can take this week?

_____

_____

_____

_____

_____

Action Step: First, make a list of two exercises that you enjoy that "feel" right for your body. Maybe you already have confidence doing them. Then, start your next workout off with those two exercises. Let them get your blood flowing and confidence up. Add additional exercises as you continually raise your own standard.

1. _____

_____

2. _____

_____

spirit
SOUL-GARDEN

9

"Let your roots grow down into him, and let your lives be built on him. Then your faith will grow strong in the truth you were taught, and you will overflow with thankfulness." – Paul, Colossians 2:7

Healthy things grow.

My wife has a garden along the side of our home. There are things that she does everyday that help the flowers and herbs to grow:

- Waters
- Removes slugs and other pests
- Adds special enriched soil
- Keeps proper spacing

But as good as she is at caring for her garden, the ultimate growth of the plants is out of her control. She did not invent the plants. She did not generate the water or tell it what to do in the soil. She did not create soil, nor does she energize its creative capacity.

She did not manufacture plant seeds or engineer their ability to open up and expand.

When it comes to the garden, there is an important role that my wife plays. And yet it seems there is a God of nature playing a critical role in the economies of life. Without some kind of mysterious miracle taking place, the creation of life is impossible.

Our spiritual lives have long been referred to in plant-like metaphor. One famous reference from the Bible is this: "The Spirit produces the fruit of love, joy, peace, patience, kindness, goodness, faithfulness, gentleness, self-control. There is no law that says these things are wrong" (Galatians 5:22-23). Notice:

1. The verse teaches that God's Spirit is ultimately responsible for producing spiritual fruit.
2. Fruit that God likes to produce includes things like love, joy, peace, patience, and kindness. I don't know anyone who hates anything on that list. They all improve the quality of our lives. They also make the lives of others more attractive.
3. No laws oppose these spiritual fruits. In fact, most of our laws exist because of them. They are a sort of baseline for "life as it should be" in almost any culture.

So we could rightly say that God is the Source of "life as it should be." He both designed life (and health and growth), and He gives us the capacity to function in ways that produce health in us, the "fruit" of which brings with it great benefit and blessing to our lives and to those around us. And yet, our world is not The Garden of Eden that perhaps it once was. Why? I think it's less about plants and trees and more about the "invisible" spiritual fruit.

I have a choice. Like my wife chooses to diligently manage her garden, I choose daily whether or not I will participate in the growth of my spiritual life, and to what degree. While, as the verse says, it's the Spirit who ultimately produces (does the miracle work), I still have a role to play.

I still make choices about the soil status. I can choose to water daily, often, or seldom. I can remove the slugs and pests that try and steal my fruit, or I can let them roam wild.

At the risk of being Captain Obvious, let's be brutally honest about the quality of spiritual fruit in your life, and talk about some practical things you can do to promote growth.

Ask yourself the following self-assessment questions. You can answer them on the next page:

- How many people regard me as a loving, joyful, patient, or kind person?
- Is my default reaction to disappointment anger or gentleness?
- Do my habits suggest that I am a person of self-control or that I am self-indulgent?
- Would my spouse, family, friends, and co-workers describe me as faithful? What is the evidence?

The "action" part of this can be dangerous. Remember what we observed: that only God's Spirit gets the credit for our spiritual growth, and yet we have a role to play. But the last thing we need are a bunch of high and mighty people thinking they are better than others because of their expert soul-gardening. Nobody likes those people. Let's do it with a humble and right view of ourselves, and gratitude toward God for causing the growth and blessings in our lives.

Here are some simple steps we can take to make and keep our lives ready for spiritual growth:

- Develop a morning ritual. Example: 1) wake up 2) pray a prayer of gratitude and dependence on God 3) read something that helps align your mind/heart with what matters most [might be Scripture] 4) exercise and eat
- Meditate on a helpful quote, thought, or Bible verse throughout the day.

- Reflect in the evening: What went well today? Where did you get off track, etc.?
- Be grateful. Gratitude is the gateway to a receptive spirit. List in the space below everything you're grateful for in your life. It can be simple things, from shoes and cereal to people and opportunities. List everything that comes to mind in the next three minutes.
- Are there any next steps that come to mind? Jot them down, too. Consider starting your day this way at least twice a week. I think it's one of the most valuable habits I practice.

"The spiritual life does not remove us from the world but leads us deeper into it." – Henri J. M. Nouwen

mind

MIND-SHIFT: LESS SELF, MORE LOVE

10

I want to briefly paraphrase a very famous story for you:

> There was a man going along the road from one major city to another. At a lonely place in the road, thieves jumped out from behind the bushes and beat the man within an inch of life, taking all his money and valuables. They left the man there to die.
>
> A few minutes later, a certain religious leader was walking that same way. Seeing the bloody mess from a ways off, he crossed to the other side of the street so he wouldn't feel obligated to stop. After all, he was a religious man, and touching someone else's blood would require him to go through a series of cleaning rituals. It would be a great inconvenience. To him, this was a complicated matter.
>
> A short time after that another religious leader—from a different tradition—walked along that same road. He, too, crossed the street to stay away from the bloody mess. He was in a hurry.
>
> Moments later, a man from an unfavorable background passed by. He saw the wounded man lying there, bloody and beaten. He had compassion on him. He felt sorry for him in spite of the fact that the wounded man was a foreigner, and, under normal circumstances, would likely despise having any interaction with this third passer-by because of his race. The prejudice between the two races ran deep.
>
> Nonetheless, this third passer-by cared for the injured man as if he were family. He spared no expense, taking him to an inn and paying the inn-keeper extra money just to look after the injured

man. He promised that if the inn-keeper incurred any further expense, he would return and pay it himself.

Jesus told this story. And since He seems to hold the outright title for the most famous and influential person to ever live, I figure it serves us to let Him challenge our ways of thinking.

When Jesus originally told the story He was talking to a group of religious leaders—who also, by the way, despised the race of the hero in the story. Imagine their frustration when Jesus challenged their comfort and their worldview.

Imagine the "elephant in the room" as the religious leaders gradually recognized that the story was being told to challenge them—that Jesus was suggesting that they were like the men who avoided the issue and didn't lend a hand. Imagine the conflicting emotions: "Whoa, is this Jesus guy suggesting that an "immoral" Samaritan from the other side of the tracks is more spiritual and more loving than I am? Could he be right? Never mind; let's just kill him and get rid of him..."

Empty religion steps over hurting people to stay "clean" and to stay on task or on "mission." But Jesus repeatedly talked about loving people, serving those in need, and giving of our resources and ourselves.

Some people have it in their minds that they are more spiritual than others because of their religious practices. Jesus might disagree.

Others think little about their spiritual health because they associate spiritual things with prideful religious people and all their rules. Jesus had one rule with two parts: LOVE... Love God; love people.

"Anyone who sets himself up as "religious" by talking a good game is self-deceived. This kind of religion is hot air and only hot air. Real religion, the kind that passes muster before God the Father, is this: Reach out to the homeless and loveless in their plight, and guard against corruption from the godless world." – James 1:26-27

How often do we ignore an obvious need around us? Perhaps it's a hurting individual, or a marginalized group of people, or even an environmental issue. Our culture tends to be heavy on tolerance, light on love. How can you spread a little love today—even if it costs you something? Here's an even bigger question: How can you engage your mind on behalf of others today?

Hint: Such actions might at first seem bold, presumptuous, and counter-cultural...but this is how things change!

_____

_____

_____

_____

_____

_____

_____

_____

_____

_____

_____

_____

_____

heart
BELIEVE THE UNBELIEVABLE

What if there were no doubts...no insecurities...nothing holding you back...what would your heart tell you to do with your life?

Growing up, I heard people say, "You can accomplish anything your heart desires. You can be anything you want to be."

That's not true.

There are some things that I can't be. No matter how hard I try, I will never be a world-class horse jockey. Those guys are a little over 5 feet tall. I'm six feet and three inches. Even if I set my mind to understanding everything there is to know about being a jockey, I would never be as good as those smaller guys. They would always weigh less than me and their horses would run faster.

Similarly, I will never be a great opera singer. I could spend the rest of my life learning everything about classical opera. I could get training from the best voice coach in the world. But the point remains: I'm not a good singer. I don't have the vocal chords. No matter how badly I want it, that's just not how God made me.

Sometimes the culture we live in, or the people we associate with, can confuse us. Infatuation can pose as passion. When we see a certain profession or activity getting praised, we can decide that we, too, should excel at that activity—after all, we want to be praised. Don't we deserve the same treatment and promotion as these others we see and hear about?

How about you? How are cultural, social, or family pressures inform-ing your perceived desires? Always remember that God has made you unique. There is something for you to do and become that is unique to you. No one can be the best version of you but you.

Think about the things you have "pursued" in your life. What are they? What has been your motivation? Or consider these questions: For what would you like to be known by others? What contribution to society would make you proud?

Answering these kinds of questions will point you in the direction of a dream—your dream.

If you were to change something about your life and your pursuits in order to focus on your heart's desire, whom would be most impact-ed? What fears stand in your way of believing that you could make real and even dramatic changes in your life?

Be realistic.

Be honest with yourself.

Be true to your design.

 Is it possible that God would want you to pursue the desires of your heart which He has created within you?

_____

_____

_____

_____

_____

_____

_____

Write out your thoughts out in the space below, maybe even in the form of a prayer expressing your heartfelt desires about your life to God, and asking for His help and direction.

_____

_____

_____

_____

_____

_____

_____

_____

_____

_____

_____

_____

"Delight yourself in the LORD and he will give you the desires of your heart." – Psalm 37:4

spirit

DISTRACTED TO DEATH

12

"Silence is the very presence of God—always there. But activity hides it. We need to leave activity long enough to discover the Presence—then we can return to activity with it." – M. Basil Pennington, O Holy Mountain

I lived with some friends for a couple months when I arrived in a new town in my twenties. I loved my friends. And, for the most part, I felt comfortable in their home. And yet I quickly observed that their lifestyle seemed built around distraction.

They would wake up together around 6:00 a.m. They'd do crossword puzzles over breakfast, only speaking if one of them got stuck on a word or to clarify the events of the day. Then they'd rush quickly off to work in a whirlwind of frantic energy.

I discovered that on the way to work, each had their own radio station of preference—in their respective cars. Work was filled with emails, meetings, and other obligations.

Between 5:00 and 6:00 p.m., both would arrive home. Immediately, local news would be on the television. She would throw together a dinner that tasted far better than the effort involved and he would pour a cocktail. After dinner, the ritual was to sit in their well-grooved chairs until the conclusion of whatever prime time television show was on that night. She would knit all evening—ever productive—while he would inevitably fall asleep in his chair before 9:00 p.m. When she was done watching and knitting, usually about 9:30 p.m., she'd wake him up and they'd both go upstairs to separate bedrooms, turn on separate televisions, and continue to watch/listen until they fell asleep. It was as if they needed the noise to rest.

These friends of mine are not unusual. And these particular individuals were in their fifties. Lifestyle-wise, the noise, media, and distraction factor goes up even higher for the younger generations.

We're living in the most technological, connected, yet distracted era in the history of humanity. Our cell phones are multimedia leashes— enslaving us to obligations and entertaining us to death, literally. In some ways, when we never slow down, never disconnect, and never get silent, we are allowing our spirits to slowly die inside of us.

I think that silence for the spirit is like water to the flower. I know that silence seems brutal for some people. But if that's the case for you, ask yourself why. If you say, "I'm a people-person," that's likely a cop-out. We all need people. So that's not really the issue. I dare say that some people use other people as a crutch, so as not to have to get to know themselves.

Every human being was given a spirit inside of him or her by our Creator. That spirit whispers of God. It whispers of greater mean- ing and significance than we currently experience. And that whisper can make us feel vulnerable, nervous, out of control, incomplete... even unproductive. But that's the point.

When we are silent and still, we are inevitably reminded that we are not ultimately in control. There is something/Someone bigger who keeps this world turning. There is someone of significant and invis- ible power who is sustaining our very breath. You didn't design your own lungs. You didn't invent oxygen.

But when we are distracted with busyness we can fool ourselves into believing that we are self-sufficient, or that we really don't need this Creator-God. We can achieve and provide for ourselves. We can try to forget or massage away our hurts and fears. We can distract and entertain ourselves to the point of numbing.

Unfortunately, the further we dull the whisper of our spirits, the closer we come to denying we have any need of God. And from all I've read and from the accounts of elder, wiser people who have gone before, it seems that's a path that ends badly.

Our spirits are our compass leading home and silence clears the way. Let's pause, and let our spirits lead.

"Be still and know that I am God." – Psalm 46:10

Identify one "distraction" activity in your daily experience that you can eliminate, or at least minimize. How will doing so help you become more attentive to your spiritual health?

_____

_____

_____

_____

_____

_____

_____

_____

body
LONG, SWEATY WALKS

13

Hydration Principle: When you're thirsty, it's too late.

Terry coached my basketball teams when I was a kid. He's in his sixties now, and doesn't play or coach basketball. Instead, he walks marathons. It's his retirement hobby. He and his wife travel all over the country going from marathon to marathon. I saw a picture of Terry walking his last marathon. He was in jean shorts and a tucked-in polo shirt. That's not my style, but I respect it.

I've talked with Terry about his hobby. He's passionate about it. He's living the glory years of retirement. And he's staying healthy doing it.

Terry has a few secrets to his marathon-marching success:

1. He keeps a good pace.
2. He keeps a good attitude.
3. He never misses a hydration station.

Any competitive long-distance athlete knows that if you reach the point of feeling dehydrated, it's too late to ask for a drink. The damage is done. You won't be able to replenish in time while your body is in constant motion. You pretty much just have to hope for the best and pop in an IV needle after the race.

This is the reason why there are hydration stations every mile or two along a marathon course. Even if Terry isn't yet thirsty, he takes a drink—because he knows dehydration creeps up on a person. Even when he's not thirsty he takes a drink, because he know his body is using up water and it's critical to his long-term success to replenish.

Now look, I'm not a marathon runner. I've done one half-marathon and never want another number on my chest. But I've included this "chewable" in our readings because I believe we can all apply this healthy "hydration principle" to our everyday lives.

There are a number of important disciplines to which we should be committed to cultivating, even when we don't feel like we need them. Some of them pertain to physical fitness; others are simply "life fitness." Here are some important healthy habits that have come up as I've talked with others:

- A glass of water every morning
- Regular exercise
- Daily vitamins
- Daily action items
- Balancing budget
- Phone call to mom (or family member)
- Support group meetings
- Sex with spouse
- Church attendance
- Regular prayer

Now it's your turn. List a couple more habits that you know are important to your overall health and that you should be doing more regularly—even if you don't feel like you're lacking yet. I offer the same encouragement that my friend Terry would offer to a wannabe marathon runner: don't wait till you're thirsty to get on top of it.

_____

_____

_____

_____

What might be one simple adjustment you can make to your schedule right now (this week) to incorporate the "hydration principle" into your life? _____

_____

_____

_____

■+ Replenish everyday.

As water is to your body, so encouragement is to your spirit. Where do you go for encouragement?

Places I go:
- Podcasts
- Uplifting TV shows/movies
- Church
- Books
- Small groups/Support Groups
- Conferences
- Inspiring People

Who are the encouraging people in your life? What can you do to make sure you have a consistent supply of encouragement along the course of your life?

_____

_____

_____

_____

_____

SIMPLE AS STRENGTH

14

"The Lord protects the simple-hearted; when I was in great need, he saved me." – Psalm 116:6

I've heard of simple-minded, but "simple-hearted" was new for me when I read the Bible verse above. The phrase brings a number of things to mind. It makes me think of a child who trusts his parents with unwavering confidence, like the way my brothers and I would leap from the top bunk of our room into our dad's arms. He'd start right on the edge of the bed and step backwards following every successful jump. By the end, and because of the strength of my 10-year-old leaping legs, he'd be halfway out the bedroom door. (Caution: before you play this game with your kids, be sure to turn off any ceiling fans. Yeah, I've lived the consequence.)

Recently, I heard a psychologist talk about the how-to's of changing one's life. He said to effect real change, we have to become more like a child. The psychologist explained that our minds get filled with negative thoughts and associations as we grow up. And in order to change, we need to break down those patterns of thinking and believing and trust—almost naively—like a child learning right from wrong.

Think about children for a minute. They trust their mother or father to meet all their needs. They don't even realize all the needs they have or all the areas in which they are dependent. They just live moment to moment, willing to be led, willing to experience life as it unfolds. Whatever happens, it is the parent who is responsible for making sense of a situation for a child. This is where things generally go wrong for kids. Parents are human, and parents grew up with imperfect parents themselves. They/we don't always handle situations well, and don't always train children in the appropriate living-giving ways.

Thus, as children grow up, they often develop crooked, biased, and negative thought patterns in their minds. Maybe dad dropped them when they leaped from the top bunk, so they think adults can't be trusted. Maybe the bed broke underneath them, so they don't trust heights. Maybe the situation was much more severe, and there are lasting scars that inhibit a healthy self-esteem.

No one can get through life without experiencing brokenness—either their own or that of others. However, if we're going to change... if we want to liberate some aspect of our lives that's been holding us back... if we want to let go of some emotional baggage and move on into a joyful and hopeful life... if we want to break out of our current rut and into a new level of potential... it's going to take faith like a child.

Can I suggest that it's time to let your heart be simple?

Yes, it can feel risky. Yes, you might get hurt or disappointed. And yes, not everyone is trustworthy. But you don't have to trust everyone.

In the same way that kids grow, develop, and build strong, healthy muscles, we all, too, need to build up our emotional muscles. First, we start just by trusting God. Here are some prayers of trust that I've prayed that have helped me build trust:

- I want to trust You... help me in my fear and doubt
- I trust You to meet my needs today
- Help me to trust that Your plan for me is good
- I trust that You know and love me
- Please make Yourself more real to me

Second, we start small, by trusting just a few select friends. You could do this by seeking out and finding one or two people whom you know value and desire to practice some of the truths contained in this book.

Keep in mind, people will inevitably let us down, just like we will inevitably let down others. But that shouldn't prevent us from being simple-hearted. The childlike response to hurt is to quickly forgive and move forward. I know, easier said than done. But it's the path to freedom.

"Let the children come to me. Don't stop them! For the Kingdom of God belongs to those who are like these children." – Jesus, Mark 10:14

Question: Looking back into your childhood, at what point do you think you stopped being able to be "childlike?" What learned behaviors have you adapted to protect yourself that might be limiting you now?

_____

_____

_____

_____

_____

_____

_____

Action: Call the most fun and childlike person you know—maybe it's your own child or a niece or nephew—and go play. Coming from someone who has taken himself too seriously at times, just doing something silly or ridiculous can actually help break the old pattern. You won't regret doing this.

OUT OF CONTEXT

15

Have you ever had a spiritual high? I used to go to camps when I was younger. I'd come back from camp all excited about life and God. I'd have made new declarations and renewed decisions. I was sure my life would be forever different—and probably, to some degree, it was. But once I was home from camp and back at school for about two weeks, the high wore off. Not just one time. Every time.

I wonder what it would be like to be a monk. I think the sacrifice, discipline and commitment their lives demonstrate is remarkable. There have been times when I've wanted to leave my life as I know it and live in a monastery on a hill in France or the Swiss Alps. It'd be serene, simple, and—in my mind, anyway—it would be a spiritual "high."

When the high wears off of a spiritual experience, a lot of people question the experience entirely. Was it real? Was it contrived? Did I get caught up in emotionalism or some kind of fake hype? I'm convinced that those "camp" kinds of experiences are very real. They are reminders of what is possible. But their lack of long-term sustainability is the normal experience of life for a reason: it is much harder work to maintain a spiritual high in context of everyday life.

And yet that is the journey. That is the daily goal.

What if we could sustain it—a spiritual high, I mean? What if a spiritual high was a reminder of what's possible for our normal lives? Not to make us all move to a hut on a hill, but to beckon us to something more...something more in the context of everyday. The reality is that spiritual growth happens in the context of life.

Spiritual highs happen on mountain tops to keep us going when we get back down to the bottom of the mountain again, and to remind us of what's possible.

Don't give up on spiritual growth because you haven't been able to sustain your high. Don't run to "spiritual activities" as if they are your only hope. They, too, can be reminders and catalysts, but they aren't the point. The point is that you can meet God anywhere.

Remember, too, that spiritual growth often happens when you aren't expecting it. It happens when you're going through hard times. It happens when you're desperate and cry out for help. It happens when you make small changes to daily habits and remind yourself regularly that God is near. Are you looking? Are you growing? You probably are.

Has your experience of mountain top-to-valley spiritual experiences disillusioned you from expecting that you can have spiritual fulfillment in the context of every day life? What are you doing to grow spiritually, just where you are? What circumstance, challenge, or crisis are you experiencing right now (or have you experienced) that might be serving the purpose of helping you grow spiritually?

_____

_____

_____

Here's an optional idea (as if something in this book were not optional). Start a spiritual journal. I recommend keeping a journal like that for a couple reasons:

- Regular reminder to reflect and examine your life
- Put words to thoughts, feelings and emotions
- Talk to God in less "weird" ways (for some people)
- Keep a record of life events, personal development, and answers to prayer

I don't journal everyday. But the seasons where I'm journaling more regularly seem to be my healthier seasons of life. And I love looking back over past journals and seeing from where I've come...and how God has met me in the context of my everyday life.

Try it.

"If we think we are going to grow in faith by sitting around at a Bible study, we are wrong. That stuff is fine, but without a story, without diving into something really difficult, something that requires us to look to God for support and wisdom and comfort, it will be more difficult to become a person of great faith." – Don Miller

heart
THE POWER OF FORGIVENESS

16

Corrie Ten Boom, a prisoner in a World War II German concentration camp called Ravensbruck, suffered greatly during the Holocaust for assisting and hiding Dutch Jews. The following is an excerpt from a story she told about having to forgive one of the guards who had been party to her torture and the death of her sister, Betsie:

"It was in a church in Munich that I saw him... It came back with a rush: that huge room with its hard overhead lights, the pathetic piles of dresses and shoes in the center of the floor, the shame of walking naked past this man. I could see my sister's frail form ahead of me, ribs sharp beneath the parchment of skin...The place was Ravensbruck, and the man who was making his way forward had been a guard—one of the most cruel guards. I would recognize him anywhere.

Now I, who had spoken so glibly of forgiveness, fumbled in my pocketbook, rather than to take that hand...He could not remember me...

'You mentioned Ravensbruck in your talk,' he was saying. 'I was a guard there. But since that time I have become a Christian. I know that God has forgiven me for the cruel things I did there, but I would like to hear it from your lips as well...will you forgive me?'

I stood there—I, whose sins had again and again needed to be forgiven—and I could not forgive. [My sister] had died in that place—could he erase her slow, terrible death simply for the asking?

It could not have been many seconds that he stood there—hand held out—but to me it seemed hours as I wrestled with the most difficult thing I had ever had to do. For I had to do it—I knew that. The message was that God forgives those who have injured us. I knew it not only as a commandment of God, but as a daily experience.

And still I stood there with the coldness clutching my heart. But forgiveness is not an emotion—I knew that, too. Forgiveness is an act of the will, and the will can function regardless of the temperature of the heart. 'Jesus, help me!' I prayed silently. 'I can lift my hand. I can do that much. You supply the feeling.'

And so woodenly, mechanically, I thrust my hand into the one stretched out to me. And as I did, an incredible thing took place. The current started in my shoulder, raced down my arm, and sprang into our joined hands. And then [God's] healing warmth seemed to flood my whole being, bringing tears to my eyes[1]."

Authentic forgiveness is radical. In order to forgive, we must determine to pay the debt of the offender, the "debt" being the sense that the other person needs to "pay" for what he or she has done. That's what Corrie did in the story above—and the result was an amazing sense of freedom and healing.

When we truly forgive—whether the other person asks us to or not—we release the offender from any obligation to us. We don't expect him or her to settle the debt; we are willing to pay the cost. It doesn't make sense from a human perspective, does it? But it has powerful effects.

Jesus said this: "If you forgive those who sin against you, your heavenly Father will forgive you. But if you refuse to forgive others, your Father will not forgive your sins" (Matthew 6:14-15). Unforgiveness can torture the person who carries it. But forgiveness brings freedom and healing.

 When do you find yourself holding grudges, erupting in anger, boiling on the inside, or just "burying" any wrongs committed against you? Whom, and in what ways, do you need to forgive?

As an exercise of commitment and follow through, write out your statement of forgiveness in the spaces below. When feelings of resentment or self-pity start to surface (and no doubt they will from time to time), come back to your written declaration and re-affirm your commitment to forgive.

_____

_____

_____

_____

_____

_____

_____

_____

_____

_____

1. Ten Boom, Corrie, "I'm Still Learning to Forgive," *Guideposts* magazine, Carmel, New York: 1972.

heart
WE NEED EACH OTHER

17

"The most I can do for my friend is simply be his friend." – Henry David Thoreau

I have a friend who's going through a divorce right now. It's painful. When I talked to him recently I could tell he was a mess. He tried to downplay it, but I knew he was on the verge of a breakdown.

"Why don't you come stay at our house tonight?" I suggested.

"No; it's okay," he declined, in a numb state of shock.

"Let me try that again. You're coming over here. Are you going to drive or am I going to pick you up?"

He pulled up twenty minutes later. We laughed, cried, ate cookies, and watched football. He thanked me as he walked upstairs to the guest room. "It wouldn't have been good for me to be alone tonight."

Why is our first instinct usually to resist others when they reach out to us? Yes, there are times to be alone. But there are also times when it's critical to be with people.

On the outside, we tend to keep people at arm's length. With our inside hand we beckon people closer. But when they get too close, or when we perceive some threat, we give them the "stiff arm" again and go back to maintaining life as we (safely) know it.

We all have pain and pressures that fuel the issue, and I can be just as messed up as the next person. But what's important today is that you and I learn to recognize self-protection when it's in our game.

I'm not talking here about not having healthy boundaries. We all need to set parameters so our lives don't get over run by the agendas and neediness of others. But I'm talking about something different, something inside us that resists being totally honest and authentic, something that builds a wall between us and the people we see every day. It works against God, too.

We're all part of one team. We're all part of one humanity. Our stories intersect, and we need each other.

 Is there someone in your life right now who needs you? Will you reach out to him or her right now?

Or is it you who's in need today?

Who in your life is "there for you" no matter what? Are you willing to be vulnerable to others and express your need for support?

If you're having trouble, here's a lead-in: "Hey... I'm kind of in a rough place in my life right now. I'm not counting on you to fix anything... I was just hoping we could hang out."

_____

_____

_____

_____

_____

_____

_____

_____

mind
YOUR LIFE'S ADVENTURE

18

"It's a dangerous business, Frodo, going out your door. You step onto the road, and if you don't keep your feet, there's no knowing where you might be swept off to." – Bilbo Baggins, *Lord of the Rings*

I had a quarter-life crisis when I was 26. I was on pace with high-achievers in life, a step ahead even. And then... Kaboom! It wasn't instantaneous. It was a slow leak of gnawing discontentment. For me, the adventure and joy of life seemed just out of reach.

I thought of that when I saw the animated film, *Up*. Have you seen it? In the movie, a grumpy old man is unsatisfied with how his life has turned out. His wife—his best friend since childhood—dies and leaves him alone in their home. He's purposeless and with no direction for his later years. He reminisces over unfulfilled dreams and hopes for a life that seems to have passed him by.

These kinds of feelings are not reserved for the elderly, as I learned for myself. Subtle feelings of regret and disappointment can lead to despair, and they can start even in the prime of your life.

That's because regret doesn't start in the body; regret begins in the mind...

- ❑ "Did I make the right decision?"
- ❑ "Why did it have to end that way?"
- ❑ "Have I ruined everything?"
- ❑ "It's their fault!"
- ❑ "I missed the boat..."

As those thoughts and questions take hold in our minds, we can fixate on them and let them negatively influence our emotions. Obviously, negative emotions cause us to feel bad. And even more obviously, our natural instinct and desire is to feel good. What's the quickest and easiest way to "feel better" when we're experiencing negative emotions? Medicate.

Enter the world of drugs and distractions. Clearly, negative emotions keep business booming for the street dealers. But there are even more ways to legally stimulate your emotions. Anti-depression and anxiety mediations are being prescribed in record numbers. In a recent study, 80% of people surveyed said that they were more likely to take a pill to deal with their depression than to seek counseling.

I get it. I've spent way too much money on counseling. And I have family members very close to me who've seemed to benefit from a little medication in the short run. But let's be honest. It's not a long-term solution. It's just a temporary "Band-Aid®." It doesn't fix the problem of negative thoughts that doom our emotions.

Back to the movie, *Up*...

When they were kids, the old man and his wife had started a journal they called their "Adventure Book." Their dream was to explore the distant and legendary "Paradise Falls." The Adventure Book was supposed to be the place where they captured all their pictures and stories of their travels, sightseeing, and explorations. But year after year, it sat on the shelf.

Instead of the pursuit of Paradise Falls, their time and money were allocated elsewhere, like to the child they dreamed of but never had, to car repairs, the mortgage, hospital bills...everyday life responsibilities. As you watch the movie, you can understand why the old man feels a sense of regret and disappointment, not only over the loss of his best friend, but also because he never provided her the adventures they had once dreamed of.

Then one day, the old man finally has the courage to pick up the Adventure Book. With a tear in his eye and regret written all over his face, he turns the page. He sees the picture of the two of them as children—so much hope, so many dreams. And now, more regret. He almost can't bear it. He starts to close the book—as if to seal his bitter fate—when another picture slides out from the bottom.

The old man turns past the initial pages to what he assumes will empty spaces, signifying the void in his life. But to his amazement, the pages are full.

First, there are photos from their wedding day. He must've known that they existed. But in their Adventure Book? And the purchase of their home. A broken limb. A new car. And so the story of their lives unfolds in front of him all over again.

Without the old man knowing, his wife had documented every stage of their lives—their adventure together. For her, **life itself** had been the great adventure. There was no Paradise Falls. But she made paradise from the life she lived.

As the shocked and humbled—and formerly grumpy—old man turns the final page, he sees his wife's handwriting. He recalls how she had requested the book one last time on her deathbed. He reads her last words to him:

"Thanks for the adventure! Now go have a new one. – Love, Ellie"

Question: What past failure, disappointment, or tragedy is weighing heavy on your mind today? What would it look like to turn the page and live a bold new adventure—to write a new story for your future?

_____

_____

_____

_____

_____

_____

_____

Action: Write down the negative thoughts—and feelings—associated with disappointment from the past. Tell yourself that the past doesn't have to dictate the future. Now write down a new thought of hope and optimism for today. Every time the old thoughts or feelings come back, train yourself to replace them with the new way of thinking that brings life and hope for future adventures.

_____

_____

_____

_____

_____

_____

_____

"I have come that they might have life, and have it to the full." – Jesus, John 10:10

spirit
REAL AND RADICAL

19

Living life in light of eternity doesn't always make sense in the physical world.

Some people stop short in their journey with God because they don't want to look weird or strange in the eyes of others. At times, I've been one of those people.

I remember how important it was for me to be perceived as "cool," or accepted by my friends and others of influence. Peer pressure is real. And the funny thing is, we don't outgrow it. We always have peers. And we will always fight the temptation to go along with the crowd and worry about what others think instead of keeping the most important things as our top priority.

Here's an observation about our peers and the pressure to conform: The people whom I thought were cool in high school seemed much less cool in college. The people whom I thought were cool in college haven't done very well in the working world. And most of the people whom I've thought were cool in culture (sports/entertainment, etc.) don't seem to stay cool long.

So why do I care if those people think I'm cool? Why did I think they were cool? I've needed to redefine "cool."

Today, the people I want to spend time with and model my life after are both real and radical. By "real" I mean genuine. These are the people who are honest. They aren't fake. They don't pretend to be something they are not. They don't pretend to be perfect. They know that they struggle with the same issues as everyone else. But they are committed to health and they desire to live lives that make a difference in the world. I think that makes them "radical."

The "radical" person is willing to disappoint the crowd to do what he or she knows is right. He (or she) is willing to make sacrifices today for the sake of tomorrow, even when tomorrow's outcome is "invisible" to some.

People who are both real and radical are typically fascinated by Jesus, since Jesus was the ultimate example of real and radical. Many of these types of people would tell you that instead of being concerned with peer pressure, they are obsessed with the priorities of God. And somehow that makes these people strangely attractive—magnetic.

Do you know anyone like this? Do you know anyone whose life is mysteriously compelling? Who, when you're with them, makes you feel like a better person—a person who is becoming both real and radical?

As one such man has told me, we need to learn to live for an audience of One. That means we need to care more about what God thinks than what anyone else thinks. That's a perspective that seems to make more and more sense to me all the time.

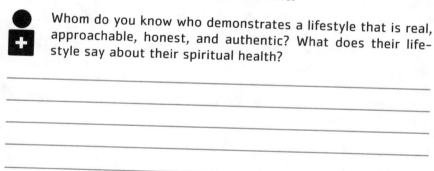

Whom do you know who demonstrates a lifestyle that is real, approachable, honest, and authentic? What does their lifestyle say about their spiritual health?

_____

_____

_____

_____

_____

Call that person and make an appointment to meet. Be authentic. Tell them that you like what you see in their life and you'd like to learn from them. It might seem awkward, but it's both real and radical—and it will pay off.

"...let us throw off everything that hinders and...let us run with perseverance the race marked out for us." – Hebrews 12:1

Have you ever seen someone running late for a flight in the airport? He (or she) is fully dressed—perhaps in a suit—and dragging along a briefcase, a purse, luggage...and maybe a child or two. It's a funny sight, someone trying to run while carrying all that extra stuff. Maybe it's the stuff that made that person late in the first place!

Contrast that image with this new one: Picture yourself running through a soft, grassy field on a sunny day...barefoot, with light, comfortable clothes. Your pace is quick but steady. You don't tire easily. The end of your race might not be in sight but that's okay, because the run is enjoyable. That's how we're supposed to run—unhindered, with nothing entangling us, slowing us down, or tripping us up.

The quote at the top of this page makes an important point. There are a lot of things that can trip us up and drag us down, things that as moral humans most of us would agree are wrong and have negative consequences—not just physical consequences but also emotional and spiritual consequences.

Some of these things we may classify as morally wrong and/or unethical. But some things may not necessarily be "bad" in and of themselves. Nonetheless, they can be detrimental to our overall health if we don't manage them properly. Here are a few examples that come to my mind of things that we easily justify as not being bad or wrong, but that still might hinder us from being healthy and from becoming all that God designed us to be:

1. Watching lots of television
2. Eating junk food
3. Sleeping too much or too little
4. Playing video games for hours on end
5. Spending excessive time in isolation
6. Spending money on unnecessary things

I'm not condemning these activities. As I said, in and of themselves they are not necessarily **wrong**. I'm just posing a question: Will they help us or hinder us on our pursuit of health?

Did any of those items jump out at you? What physical distractions are slowing you down on your journey toward health? How can you eliminate some activities that may not be "bad," but which distract you from becoming the person you want to be?

_____

_____

_____

_____

Choose one—one aspect of your life that's not necessarily bad, but probably not helpful or healthy, either. For me, I've been thinking about how much time I spend watching sports on TV. I'm not going to give it up entirely, but I've decided to DVR (record) games and watch them without commercials. And I'm going to limit the time I spend on the couch. How about you? _____

_____

_____

_____

mind
THE BATTLE FOR THE MIND

"The mind is like an iceberg; it floats with one-seventh of its bulk above water." – Sigmund Freud

Every action starts in the mind.

There was a study done with two basketball teams that were considered to be of the same skill level and experience. The two teams had played each other in the past and the games were always close, with both teams winning equally as often. In the study, they were set to play each other again but this time they were to prepare very differently.

Team One practiced in the gym every day for a week leading up to the game. Team Two didn't practice at all. Instead, they went into a classroom and just talked about how they were going to beat the other team. They went through their plays in their minds. They pictured themselves sinking baskets, making passes, and playing great defense. They conditioned themselves to win the game, but only mentally. They didn't pick up a basketball all week.

The outcome? Team Two—after practicing only in their minds for a week—beat Team One convincingly. The next time, the experiment was reversed, but the outcome was the same. The team that spent the week preparing mentally outperformed the team that only practiced physically.

Our minds are mysteriously powerful.

Consider all the things that cross your mind on a daily basis. The National Science Foundation suggests that the average person thinks about 12,000 thoughts per day. A deeper thinker might have up to 50,000 thoughts daily.

The natural question is: What are **you** thinking about? Are those thoughts pushing you into the future you want, or are they deterring, distracting, and discouraging you?

Our minds have incredible power. They govern our thoughts, our attitudes, our perspectives, and our approach to any given situation. It makes sense that we would protect our minds. It also makes sense that we would want to prepare our minds to serve us, and to stay healthy for life.

"Therefore, prepare your minds for action..." – 1 Peter 1:13

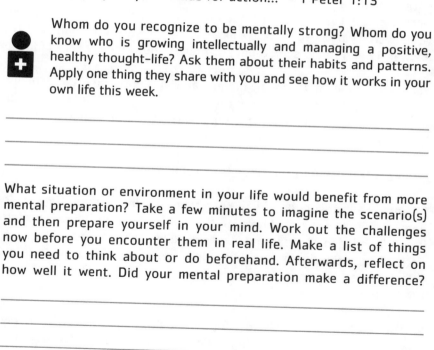

Whom do you recognize to be mentally strong? Whom do you know who is growing intellectually and managing a positive, healthy thought-life? Ask them about their habits and patterns. Apply one thing they share with you and see how it works in your own life this week.

What situation or environment in your life would benefit from more mental preparation? Take a few minutes to imagine the scenario(s) and then prepare yourself in your mind. Work out the challenges now before you encounter them in real life. Make a list of things you need to think about or do beforehand. Afterwards, reflect on how well it went. Did your mental preparation make a difference?

INTO THE LIGHT

Secrets kill.

Have you ever had an experience where your deepest, darkest secrets were exposed and you were humiliated? Most of us avoid that scenario like the plague. I did. Until I couldn't.

I still remember being picked up from the airport by my friend Ty. We went straight to a Mexican restaurant, but we didn't end up eating very much. Ty proceeded to ask me probing questions no man likes to answer. Ty had found something out that I'd intentionally kept hidden.

You see, I thought I was an honest and authentic guy. But I really wasn't. I was 95% authentic, but there was another 5% that I preferred to keep to myself. That 5% is the ugly stuff—the stuff you wish wasn't true about you.

So I kept it hidden. But it made the problem worse.

Secrets are like wounds. If you keep them totally covered, they can't heal. They're like the cut I have on the back of my foot. I have to keep it well-bandaged to wear shoes—especially when I exercise. But I've noticed that the cut is not improving. It's staying raw and aggravated. There is not enough oxygen getting to the wound to speed up the healing.

So I've worked out a solution. Since I can't completely stay off my feet, I wear the bandage during the day. But I'm taking a few days off from working out, and I'm letting the wound breathe every hour I'm at home—in a safe place.

Parallel: The whole world doesn't need to see our wounds. But we all need a safe place to air our secrets—because we all need to heal.

That day with Ty it became clear to me that secrets can ruin my life. Having a safe place to air them out and heal has made all the difference in the world.

So why do we keep our struggles to ourselves? And why do we pretend they are not as bad as they likely are? Because we are ashamed—and it's nothing new. Shame has been common to every human from the beginning. Just as our original ancestors, Adam and Eve, found out after what's referred to as the "original sin," shame makes us want to run and hide (see Genesis 3). It makes us feel alone, naked, corrupt, and exposed. It makes want to hide from others, and from God.

Shame is like a wet blanket hanging over our shoulders, weighing us down with guilt for past mistakes and present insecurities. Shame keeps life's struggles in the dark. In the dark, our minds get clouded by doubt and defeat, and our hearts can be overcome by despair.

Shame imprisons our hearts and makes us feel condemned—but God wants to change that. Jesus said we're supposed to be living life to the full—and that He can help: "The thief's purpose is to steal and kill and destroy. But My purpose is to give life in all its fullness" (John 10:10).

Have you ever sensed a force that's interested in stealing, killing, and destroying? That's the enemy of God. And one of his chief tactics is to make us feel shameful about our wounds and failures. That way we never come clean, we never heal, and we never experience life in all its fullness. The solution is to bring our behaviors, our thoughts, our regrets, our addictions, and our abuses into the light.

Find a safe place—and start to heal.

 "Confess your sins to each other and pray for each other so that you many be healed." – James 5:16

We all have things we wish were not true about us, or about our past. All people struggle and fail—and they always have. The Apostle Paul once said, "I do not understand what I do. For what I want to do I do not do, but what I hate I do" (Romans 7:15).

I can relate, can you? Being honest with ourselves and others opens the door to healing and health. Hope can be renewed and forgiveness received.

With whom will you meet this week and share honestly about your wounds and weaknesses? Allow them to do the same with you, if they want.

_____

_____

_____

_____

_____

_____

_____

"Thirsty hearts are those whose longings have been wakened by the touch of God within them." – A.W. Tozer

spirit
THE BIGGER QUESTION

23

"(We) are really involved with God. He's always been like, I don't know, He's held our family together. We grew up with not a lot of money, my mum and I. She was young when she had me. We struggled, but we never blamed Him." – Justin Bieber

Yes, I just quoted Justin Bieber. I like the kid. And, apparently, so does most of the under-forty-English-speaking world.

Today, Justin Bieber is a 16-year-old international pop star with mind-blowing popularity. He has the poise, personality, and talent of a brilliant veteran entertainer, yet with childlike innocence that endears him to adults and their children alike.

Look again at the quote above. The maturity comes out as he holds back details about his mother and their rough beginnings. Justin is clear that God is not to blame, and neither is his "mum." And yet it's his childlike love of God that entered into this discussion with a USA Today reporter to begin with.

Everybody has to decide how involved God will be in his or her life. Yes, I believe it's a decision. You will interpret God's activity based on the decisions you make and the beliefs you hold.

If you don't want God in your life, then all the good that happens will be because you created it. And all the bad things that happen will reinforce your belief that you don't need God—that He's not for you but against you.

Then again, if you decide that life is better connected to God, you'll find reason after reason to be grateful toward Him. You'll even learn to appreciate the hard seasons of life—and not blame Him—because they'll prepare you for the next season of life and make the good times that much better.

I'm on an airplane as I type. Traveling at 30 thousand feet above the ground has become normal. I do it regularly. But it's at times like this that I'm reminded I'm not in control of my life. At this moment, I've surrendered control to a couple of pilots and flight attendants whom I've never met and know nothing about. I'm trusting that the crew on the ground got this aircraft ready to go, and that they didn't overlook anything critical to the flight. I know nothing about what makes this plane ready to fly, or how to get it where it needs to go. I just sit here and try to sleep.

Similarly, the weather is completely out of the control of the pilots and their airline. They have no say in whether or not there is turbulence or stormy weather. All they can hope to do is avoid the rough spots. But ultimately, they are not in control.

There are countless other elements that are out of my hands. For instance, whether or not someone on the flight is a crazy person. Someone that sits next to me might have a mental illness, a vendetta, a death wish, or just diarrhea. And who determines, anyway, the person who sits next to me? Is it just chance? Does it matter at all in the scheme of life?

Again, the bigger question: Is God involved?

Did He want Justin Bieber to be zillionaire at 16? I don't know. But I think Justin would say that God is somehow involved. I think Justin realizes that he didn't make himself what he is. He didn't create YouTube—the tool that propelled him into the public eye. Neither did he create his own lungs or give himself abilities.

We can't be our own source of life. Nor are we ultimately in control. God IS involved.

And yet, we kind of are in control—of a lot of things. We are in control of how involved we allow God to be in our hearts, minds, and daily lives. We are in control of the decisions we make.

Let's call it the "human-divine cooperative." Somehow, the decisions we make coincide with how God wired the universe and produce outcomes. It's mysterious. And yet it's real. Our ultimate control is limited. And yet our decisions still shape our destinies.

"But the basic reality of God is plain enough. Open your eyes and there it is!" – Romans 1:19

Do you tend to think of yourself as being "in control" of your life? How does that play out day-to-day? _____

_____

_____

_____

When it comes to your daily decisions, what would it look like to "cooperate" with God and how He's created you and the entire universe? What do you know of God and His principles to live by?

_____

_____

_____

_____

How can you start to allow Him more involvement in your day-to-day life and decision-making? _____

_____

_____

_____

_____

 body
DESIGNED DISTINCTLY

24

My friend Jeff appreciates the uniqueness of his body. Jeff has Down syndrome, which can be readily seen in his physical appearance. But Down syndrome is not a downer for Jeff. He is confident in how God made him.

One morning, when Jeff was a teenager, he was upstairs alone in his bathroom and his mother heard him talking to himself. She slowly made her way upstairs to see if he was in need of help. As Jeff's mom approached his slightly-open bathroom door, she saw Jeff standing on top of his bathroom counter in his "tighty-whities" (underwear), triumphantly posing in front of the mirror in all his glory. Not realizing he had company, Jeff stood atop his counter— champion of his bathroom—content with his physical shape. Striking a pose with arms flexed, one leg extended, he said with admiring affection, "Thank you, ThighMaster!"

Jeff appreciated the way God made him. He wasn't looking at the world's definition of a "perfect" body in that mirror. He was looking at reality.

You won't see Jeff on the cover of health magazines or in fragrance commercials. But those things don't matter to Jeff. They don't even cross his mind. Jeff understands something that many people never figure out: we are who we are for a reason.

What do **you** think about **your** body? If you're like most people, you compare your body to some airbrushed "ideal" you've seen in magazines or on TV. Is that helpful motivation?

The fact is, our culture sells discontentment. That's because as long as you and I are discontent, we'll spend more money to try and feel better. So advertisements and media provoke our dissatisfaction with ourselves. The result is that we spend our lives pursuing an impossible ideal—and they make lots of money. Thousands of dollars, surgeries, and tears later, we're still unhappy.

The truth is that God designed you unlike any other human who has ever lived or will ever live. You are unique! And you're unique for a reason. Do you believe it?

I want to ask a question that might, on the surface, seem unrealistic or grossly idealistic. But please indulge me... What if we led a revolution? Us—simple people, with regular lives, connected by our humanity and convicted about our culture's irresponsible intrusion on our health—physical, mental, emotional, and spiritual. What if we, by our own individual choices and actions, could collectively have an impact on our culture? And what if we, as individuals, became more whole and healthy in the process? What if...?

I believe it's possible. And it can start today. It can start by thinking a little bit differently about your body.

 How do you think popular culture (media, values, expectations, commercial advertising, etc.) works against your ability to be comfortable with how you look physically?

_____

_____

_____

_____

"I praise you because you made me
in an amazing and wonderful way.
What you have done is wonderful.
I know this very well.
You saw my bones being formed
as I took shape in my mother's body.
When I was put together there,
you saw my body as it was formed.
All the days planned for me were
written in your book
before I was one day old."
The Bible, Psalm 139:13-16

If you were to make a commitment—emotionally, mentally, and spiritually—to the idea expressed in the passage above (that God designed you, created you, intentionally planned for you, knows you, and thinks you're wonderful just the way you are), how might that change the way **you** see **yourself**?

_____

_____

_____

_____

_____

_____

_____

_____

_____

mind
SOME RE-WIRING REQUIRED

25

"Men are not prisoners of fate, but prisoners of their own minds."
– Franklin D. Roosevelt

There's a scene from Episode Four of *Star Wars* where Obi-Wan Kenobi trains Luke Skywalker to be a Jedi Knight. As he begins the training, Obi-Wan tells young Luke, "I must untrain you to train you."

I'm struck by how true that is for all of us. Sometimes we need to untrain our minds to train them properly. Empty some of the garbage in there to fill it up with better stuff.

Ever feel like you need a mental detox? I certainly do.

One reason is because we live in a society that feeds us a lot of mixed messages and half-truths. Should she be a size "0" or an athlete? Should he be at home more or make millions of dollars? Should she have a career or just bigger breasts? Should he drive a nicer car or just be a nicer guy?

Culture tells us so many things about how we should live, look, and behave. Subtly, and often subconsciously, our minds slowly conform to the ways of the world around us. When it gives us positive messages, that's a good thing. But when it gives us the not-so-positive ones, well, that's a problem.

Think about the friends you had when you were younger. Even those of us who would consider ourselves leaders still went along with the crowd in some ways. And where was the crowd going? Where is the crowd going today? Whether the elementary school playground, the high school parking lot, the college fraternity, or the work place, there has been—and still is—a crowd you're going along with. The question is, where is it taking you?

If you want to make changes in your life—and you can—it all starts in the mind. And if you want to achieve new or different results, in terms of health and life in general, it's likely time for a new strategy and a new way of thinking.

Before you can establish and start living out the new healthy patterns you desire, you might have to honestly identify the old ways of thinking (and following) that were getting you nowhere. You might have to be "untrained" before you can be "trained!"

Consider the following areas of life. Take a few minutes to think long and hard, and examine your perspectives. Identify something you believe about which issue might be influencing you negatively and could use a change. Write that it down. Then identify how you would like to think about or perceive that issue. Write that down, too. Then come back to this page from time to time over the next several weeks as you work through this book. It's a great place to start.

Life Issue	Current Thinking	Re-Thinking
Body Image		
Money		
Career		
God		
Friendships		
Family relationships		
Dating/Marriage		
Parenting		
Leisure Time		

Consider the following thought from the Bible and use it to help you answer the following questions: "Do not conform any longer to the pattern of this world, but be transformed by the renewing of your mind. Then you will be able to test and approve what God's will is—his good, pleasing and perfect will." – Romans 12:2

How often do you think about God's will related to your life? Is that idea on your radar? How might knowing God's will be helpful in your current life circumstances? What are some ways you might seek that out? Some people find that talking with others, praying, meditating, reading Scriptures, attending services, and spending time out in nature can all be helpful ways to connect with God and renew their minds.

_____

_____

_____

_____

_____

_____

_____

_____

_____

_____

_____

_____

_____

_____

spirit
A VISION OF THE INVISIBLE

26

"Life is preparation for eternity." – Rick Warren

There is a spiritual realm that is as real as the physical.

I once heard a man compare the invisible reality of God to the wind. I'll paraphrase: "God is mysterious. His Spirit is at work in us, and all around us, though His Spirit is invisible. He's like the wind. I've seen the effects of the wind, but I've never seen the wind. There's a mystery to it."

And mystery is okay.

If we could understand God in His entirety, what kind of a God would He be? Not very impressive. We can't even begin to come close to comprehending how big, powerful, good, and loving God is. We can't completely understand the way He works, the things He does, or the things He doesn't do. If we could then we might confuse ourselves, thinking that we were on His level.

We cannot understand Him completely because He's so mysterious—but we can know Him personally. In fact, He reveals Himself to us in small ways all the time: "Ever since God created the world, His invisible qualities, both His eternal power and His divine nature, have been clearly seen; they are perceived in the things that God has made. So...people have no excuse at all" (Romans 1:20).

Do you remember having any "God-moments?" Anything that has happened to you or someone you love that was outside of the realm of your understanding? Anything that you just know, in the core of who you are, must've been God?

Has God been trying to get your attention? Has He been revealing Himself to you? Have you been missing Him?

It's easy to get distracted by the physical demands of the world around us and miss the more important spiritual realities that have eternal implications. Jesus pointed this out, saying "But you shouldn't be so concerned about perishable things like food. Spend your energy seeking the eternal life that I, the Son of Man, can give you. For God the Father has sent me for that very purpose" (John 6:27).

The Bible teaches that Jesus was the visible expression of the invisible God (Colossians 1:15). That means that when we look at Jesus, we get a really good picture of what God is like. How much do you know about Jesus? Studying Jesus Christ is the best way to explore who God is and how He desires us to live.

Who is Jesus to you? If Jesus is the visible representation of God, what does that tell you about God? _____

_____

_____

_____

Why do you think people have misconceptions about who Jesus is?

_____

_____

_____

_____

To study specifically about Jesus, the best source is the New Testament of the Bible. I recommend starting with the books of Luke and John.

heart
HEALTH MEANS HEALING

27

"Pain can be a great teacher when we learn to listen." – healing member of the Y

The Y member who made the above statement was sharing a personal story. Here is part of it:

"While going through a terrible relational break-up I got drastically ill and almost died of heart failure. It also affected my mind and I nearly had a nervous breakdown because of the inner turmoil I had held inside for so many years. After about a year I remember looking into the mirror one day, asking myself if I wanted to heal through this experience or continue having a pity party. There could be no blaming anyone else. This was all about me.

I realized that I needed God to help me in the process. He took me on journey back into my childhood where I had to deal with issues that have been plaguing me my whole life. I began to allow myself to cry about what had happened to me when I was a child. As God began the emotional healing I remember a nurse talking with me about joining the YMCA.

I said, 'What does exercise have to do with my healing process?' She explained that I needed a heart workout—in more ways than one. I learned that when you are being healed, your whole self needs to be a part of the process.

Because of this journey, I learned how to love myself. Now I am able to be loved and share my love with other people. God really does turn ashes into beauty."

This amazing Y member is not alone. You can't live very long in this world without experiencing pain. Pain is real. Regardless of what type of pain of it is, we need to be honest about the impact it has on all of us. When we're not honest, we become the walking wounded. Many of us are walking around with injuries that Band-Aids® won't fix. Many of us have unhealthy hearts.

The heart is more than a muscle. In many cultures, it symbolically represents the essence of who we are. It informs our emotions. It gets electrified in love. We wonder if it can break when we're rejected. It seems to learn from the past and attempt to protect itself. It gets nervous with change. The heart prefers to be open, available, "childlike," and hopeful but it also has the capacity to harden and close off, which has a general "numbing" effect on our whole self.

Just as the muscle-heart pumps blood throughout the body, the "soul-heart" pumps life and health throughout your entire being. If you don't feel energized and alive, it's time to take a closer look at the heart.

 "Above all else, guard your heart, for it is the wellspring of life." – Proverbs 4:23

Emotions are indicators. To ignore your emotions is to deny reality. To listen to and learn from your emotions ushers in a healthy reality.

When you think about your heart and your deepest feelings, what issues keep coming to the surface no matter how hard you may try to block them out? What steps will you take to allow them to surface in a safe place so you can deal with them in a healthy, healing way?

_____

_____

_____

_____

_____

mind
OUT OF AUTOPILOT

28

"We spend our health building our wealth. Then we desperately spend our wealth hanging on to our remaining health." – Robert T. Kiyosaki

The statement above is depressingly true, and it's evidence of a shallow and broken system. But it doesn't have to be your story.

So much of our life is in autopilot. We go along with the prescribed program. We settle for "normal." Our routines form themselves, then we look back months—even years—later and wonder how we got here.

Maybe we see a movie, read a book, or hear a story that reminds us that there is more. We can live differently. We can enjoy our lives more than we currently are. We can spend more quality time with our loved ones. We can pause, reflect, and dream a new dream. This is another one of those opportunities.

Give yourself a grade (A – F) in the following areas of health. Notice that I'm not prescribing a standard. This is just based on your current standard for yourself:

Physical
____ Movement/flexibility
____ Diet
____ Energy/endurance

Mental
____ Empowering thoughts
____ Challenge/development
____ Awareness/sharpness

Emotional
_____ Forgiveness
_____ Openness to relationship
_____ Confidence

Spiritual
_____ Sense of purpose
_____ Peace/Hope
_____ Connection to God

The goal of this book is to help inspire you—in large or small ways —to take steps of growth in those areas. Notice that "work performance" is not a scoring category above. Why? Because our cultural norm is to score based on achievement and performance, usually to the exclusion of our health and well-being.

I am completely convinced that growth, progress, and performance are by-products of health. Healthy things grow. Happy people perform.

Many people reading this book are people of action—people managing others, leaders and influencers in homes, businesses, schools and communities. If that describes you, how much more important is it for you to manage your health now? What you do for yourself impacts others.

There is no convenient time to switch out of autopilot and begin to make intentional changes in one's life. It's much less overwhelming, though, if we do it by tweaking small habits that we do everyday. Think about what you're doing. Then make the determination to do something different and follow through with it. It's simple—though not always easy. But it's possible. And it works.

Question: If you can articulate your "autopilot" mindset related to health, what is it? What small deliberate changes could you make that would switch you out of autopilot into a mode of intentionality?

_____

_____

_____

_____

_____

_____

_____

_____

_____

_____

_____

Action: Show the grades you gave yourself above to someone else. Tell him or her where you want to be three months from now. Ask him (or her) to check back with you at that time and ask you how you're doing.

"Your first and foremost job as a leader is to raise your own energy level and then to help raise and orchestrate the energies of those around you." – Peter Drucker

body
BUSYBODIES

29

A young girl went to her father in the front room of their house with eager anticipation. Her father was sitting in his chair, reading the newspaper. That was his routine, and he didn't have long until he was expected at work. The young girl tapped on the pages of the newspaper. With great enthusiasm she asked him to play hide-and-seek.

"Come on, Daddy! I'm going to go hide; you have to come find me."

Her father lowered his paper just long enough to respond, "Okay, honey. Go hide...I'm coming right after you."

The little girl ran with great excitement throughout the house looking for the perfect place to hide. The "perfect place" was not far away. She wanted to hide but, more than that, she wanted to be found.

After several minutes behind the piano in the next room, the little girl stuck her feet out in the open, just in case she was hiding too well. After several more minutes, she started to make some soft noises—clearing her throat, even humming. Still, her father didn't find her.

Finally, after what seemed like an eternity to the little girl, she got up from behind the piano and slowly walked into the front room. To her devastation, her father was sitting exactly where she left him—on his chair, reading the paper. She was heartbroken.

As this story sadly illustrates, busyness and distraction can cause us to miss out on life. Some of us think that a hectic pace, the tendency to be late, or a state of continual distraction is only a personal issue. But in reality, it's affecting the people around us, and often causing us to miss out on the things that matter most.

Some of us live life at break-neck speed, and never even have time to consider living another way. We never slow down long enough to realize there's a serious problem, or that our health is at risk—not to mention the health of our relationships. Others of us have plenty of time on our hands, yet we still manage to distract ourselves from doing the things of highest importance.

In many ways that mindset is driven by the culture we live in. We operate in a world that tries to tell us that our value is linked to our position—at work or socially. If we're busy, we're important. If we have money, we're significant. If we have big plans, we're going places. Everything around us seems to affirm this independent, live-for-yourself attitude. But how's it working out for us?

The United States is more crowded than it's ever been, yet survey after survey has indicated that we are more isolated, lonelier, and more depressed than any generation before us. The reason is this: We were never meant to live for ourselves. We are meant to live in community.

Think about the people who have been most significant in your life. Why are these people significant to you—and you to them? How's your distraction level when it comes to making time to cultivate these relationships?

Legacies that last are built on love for others. It's never too late to leave a legacy of love. You can start right now.

"It's not enough to be busy, so are the ants. The question is, what are we busy about?" – Henry David Thoreau

Who are the significant people and relationships in your life? Are you making time for them? Write their names below, along with some concrete strategies for making the health of your relationships as important a priority as the health of your body (or your bank account, your career, or whatever else dominates your priorities).

_____

_____

_____

_____

_____

With whom are you connecting on a regular basis? Who is supporting you in your health goals? Health is not just a personal issue. It impacts those around us—even and especially our closest relationships. We need one another. I encourage you to share your decisions and goals toward health with at least one other person—preferably a small group of people.

_____

_____

_____

_____

_____

Together, we keep pressing on.

spirit
SPIRIT FOOD

30

Someone has said, "You are what you eat."

If that is at all true physically, it is even more true spiritually, which begs the question, "What are you feeding your spirit?"

If someone is trying to prevent weight gain, it's usually better that he or she doesn't eat fatty food, or food in large quantities, especially later in the evening. So it is with the spirit. There are things we shouldn't participate in if we want to our spirits to be healthy and connected to God.

There are images and ideas that we should try to avoid putting in our minds. There are places we should try to stay away from if they make us vulnerable to temptation and/or bad choices. There are decisions that will make our spirits more or less healthy.

This not a legalistic discussion, but realistic.

If we're making a pie, we need the basic ingredients: flour, berries, sugar, etc. If we put Spam® in our berry pie, we might offend some people and make them sick.

Similarly, most cars still run on gasoline. What happens if you put lemonade in the gas tank?

Our bodies need real food. Our minds need real knowledge. Our hearts need real love. And our spirits need a real God. "It is only our own spirit within us that knows all about us...only God's Spirit knows all about God. We have...received the Spirit sent by God, so that we may know all that God has given us" (1 Corinthians 2:11-12).

What have you been feeding your spirit lately? Can you tell the difference between healthy and unhealthy spiritual food yet?

 The verse above says that God's Spirit communicates to us about who God is. Do you have any experience with this? Do you believe that you can receive from God?

Jesus said, "Man does not live on bread alone, but on every word that comes from the mouth of God" (Matthew 4:4).

What would it look like to live off the words of God?

_____

_____

_____

_____

_____

What old ways of living (or thinking) might have to change in order to consistently receive input from God?

_____

_____

_____

_____

_____

Keep reading Luke and John from the New Testament. Read small portions at a time and ask yourself these questions:
- What does this tell me about God?
- What does this teach me about me?
- What do I need to do about it?

mind
I WOKE UP

"Prayer is our humble answer to the inconceivable surprise of living. It is all we can offer in return for the mystery by which we live."
– Abraham Joshua Heschel

My wife, Hilary, wakes up happy most of the time. It's part of her child-like nature that I love and learn from. Whether it's in the morning or from a nap—it doesn't matter—she'll greet the world once again, "I woke up!"

I might be asleep still, or reading, or watching television. But it makes me smile when I hear the gentle but cheerful, "I woke up!" An announcement. I'm awake. Pay attention. I'm here. And I thought you should know.

What if every morning was like coming out of the womb and into existence again? Just less messy and awkward. "Whoa... I'm awake. This is cool." Then you immediately start talking to God, because... what else would you do?

"So...I'm alive. Life didn't discontinue while I slept. Time—whatever that is—marches on. And it feels like I'm starting over. Thanks, God."

"I suppose there's purpose for me today. I guess You, God, might have an opinion about the focus of my day..."

Then the mystery of all things Good summons your heart and mind like a compass. So you follow: "Well, let's start with what I know...You're God. I'm human. You gave me life. I feel compelled to thank You. And I feel compelled to add value to the lives You've given others around me." Then details about immediate obligations and opportunities enter the picture, but in the appropriate scope of what really matters. After all, you're alive.

Every day is a new start. And every day can be a new adventure, if we simply adapt that attitude.

Maybe it partly depends on how you wake up. Try something new this week. Keep a journal or notebook or note card next to your bed. As soon as you wake up, write down the thoughts that are filling your mind. Do you wake up hopeful and excited? Are you grateful for the gift of another day? Or is your experience more typical of Americans: overwhelmed, anxious, even bored? Write down your feelings. Think about your thoughts. What's happening underneath what's happening?

As you're getting ready for work, or for your day, consider why you woke up feeling/thinking like you did. What have you been trained to believe about life that causes—even the moment you wake up—those ideas flood your perception of this new day?

Here are some thoughts and feelings that I've identified in my own "waking mind:"

- I slept until 7:00 a.m. – I'm already behind
- Why did I watch that stupid show last night?
- What's on the calendar for today?
- I don't feel like working out
- I need better clothes
- I could stand to lose five pounds

Granted, these thoughts from a past week of wake-ups are not overly critical or depressing. One might even suggest that they're "fine" or "normal." But I want a new normal. I want to wake up with passion and energy and enthusiasm. I know this to be true because I've done it before and those have been great days. They are days filled with gratitude for being alive, hope for whatever the day may bring, and love for people instead of just tolerance.

Practice thanking God for being alive, right now. And let that be a new habit, the first thing you do every morning. We're creating new normals. And we're improving the quality of our lives.

It's a journey beneath the surface... a journey with that inner child... a journey toward a simple, hopeful life.

"You plus God equals enough." – Zig Ziglar

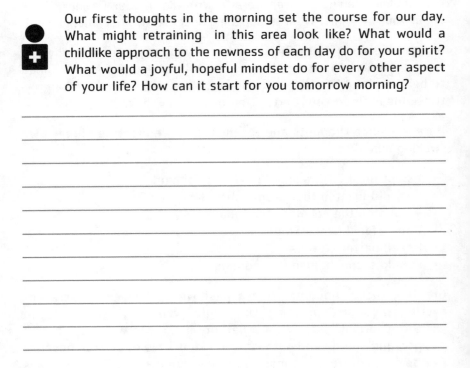

Our first thoughts in the morning set the course for our day. What might retraining in this area look like? What would a childlike approach to the newness of each day do for your spirit? What would a joyful, hopeful mindset do for every other aspect of your life? How can it start for you tomorrow morning?

body
MADE TO MOVE

32

"It is confidence in our bodies, minds, and spirits that allows us to keep looking for new adventures, new directions to grow in, and new lessons to learn..." – Oprah Winfrey

Your arms swing forward. Your eyes are on the front of your face. Your feet point ahead of you. Your mouth speaks in the direction you are facing.

We were created for action. We were designed for advancement.

The first instruction God ever gave humans was this: "Prosper! Reproduce! Fill Earth! Take charge! Be responsible for fish in the sea and birds in the air, for every living thing that moves on the face of Earth" (Genesis 1:28). In other words, "Go forward, procreate, and manage My creation!" It's our responsibility, as humans, to stay active, manage responsibly, and move creation forward. And that includes our own physical bodies.

We should be honest with ourselves about the fact that we won't live forever. Sometime in the not-too-distant future, our bodies will start to fail us. We won't be able to lift as much weight as we used to. We won't be able to run as far as we once did. Parts of us will sag and wrinkle despite our best efforts. That's just life. It is a constant reminder that we are more spiritual than we are physical. But, in terms of the physical, we can maximize what we have for the amount of time we have it.

Think about it: If you don't eat food, you'll die in a couple months. If you don't drink water, you'll die in a couple days. If you don't breathe oxygen, you'll die in a couple minutes. Similarly, if you don't work your muscles, they will atrophy (break down). If you don't exercise, your lungs will shrink. Our bodies are amazing. They will build up if we make them—or they will break down if we let them.

So, what keeps you moving? What gets you up in the morning? What are your primary motivations for what you do any given day? Is it the pursuit of happiness? Or the pursuit of "hotness" (attractiveness)? Are you chasing after wealth or significance? If so, are you satisfied with the chase?

Maybe you're not pursuing anything, and you're feeling stagnant— stuck—like you're merely existing. Before you can move forward, you first have to be honest about where you are...and then have a vision for where you want to go.

And maybe, just maybe, you feel like you've not been moving forward, but rather sliding backward. Here are a few "slide" warning signs:

1. Feeling like you're always behind
2. Waking up consistently tired
3. Blaming others for current circumstances
4. Giving up hope for the future

Many of us will admit that our lifestyle is in somewhat of a "rut," and not moving in the direction we'd like or at the pace we'd want. But change is possible! And small changes can make a big difference to get you moving forward again.

Whether you're needing to move forward, move faster, or simply just start moving again, it's not going to be enough just to "show up" at work, at home, or at the gym. You need a plan. And you need to execute the plan if you want to see change.

Don't get discouraged at this point if you don't think of yourself as the planning type. The plan doesn't have to be elaborate or complex. It can be very simple—as simple as you want. The point is to be intentional...and to move forward!

 "All we have to decide is what to do with the time we are given." – Gandalf, *Fellowship of the Rings*

Remember, we all make time for the things we value most. If you're not finding time for good health, self-care, and exercise, it's probably not yet a high enough priority. How do your priorities need to change in order to consistently take time to train your body?

_____

_____

_____

_____

_____

With whom could you partner to help you stay motivated and make physical activity more enjoyable? What might that look like?

_____

_____

_____

_____

_____

"Prayer is a relationship; half the job is mine." – Elizabeth Gilbert, *Eat, Pray, Love*

Do you have a close friend who lives far away but with whom, when you're back together, you pick up where you left off like no time has past? Those are great friends. The same jokes are still funny. There's no drama, and who called who last is irrelevant. The time is void of awkwardness and fake conversation. It's real and easy.

I'm convinced talking to God could and should be that way. I've experienced it at times. But not always.

A lot of the time it's like talking to a grandparent. I know they love me unconditionally, but I don't want to disappoint them and I wonder if they'd understand or care about the details of my life.

I heard a wonderful "grandparent" story today. A grandpa was watching his granddaughter. He put her in the back seat of his car, buckled her in, and took her for a drive. She talked the whole way. Grandpa smiled, laughed, asked questions...and loved every second of it.

After their excursion—including a park and ice cream—grandpa brought the happy little girl home. She gave him a big hug and they talked about the next time they'd see each other.

The next day, Grandpa was cleaning out his car. He always went to the same fifty-cent-vacuum-yourself place. Pulling his car alongside the hose and starting with the front seats, he worked his way to the back seat. When he opened the back door he immediately saw two miniature footprints on the floor mat, perfect little dirt impressions left by his beloved granddaughter after a glorious hour at the park. Grandpa stood there staring at the prints. Hose in hand, meter running, he stood frozen, remembering. Another minute went by and the vacuum shut itself off. Grandpa hadn't finished his back seat.

It's a month later, and Grandpa still hasn't cleaned the back floor mat. He's intentionally tried to preserve the precious memory of his cherished hours with his granddaughter. Every time he places anything in the back seat, he looks down and smiles.

I wonder if, at least in some ways, God looks at our prayers like that. I wonder if He simply cherishes the time. Maybe it's doesn't matter what we talk about, what state of mind we're in, or how dirty our feet are. Maybe He just loves when we care enough to sit and talk.

To suggest that God is like a grandpa is obviously incomplete. But it gets us part of the way there. If God is the architect of relationships then it's not a stretch to believe that in some mysterious way, everything good and healthy about relationships weaves together in some cosmic tapestry to give us a shadow of our ultimate connection to our Maker. God's essence is about relationship. God is love. Any pure and loving thing you've experienced has its origin in the Divine.

That may sound far away. Another way to look at it might be this: grandpa + best friend + lover + cool neighbor + generous stranger + favorite coach = thin slice of God's capacity to love you.

When I think like that, prayer becomes less forced and more...real.

Question: What does prayer mean to you? What have been your most recent experiences?

_____

_____

_____

_____

_____

_____

_____

_____

_____

_____

_____

_____

_____

_____

Action: Practice having a conversation with God. Try and get your mind around the idea that He cares...and that He might even talk back.

mind
MIND OVER MATTERS

34

When I turned 16 years old, my dad had all the men in my life—friends and family—write me a letter about "becoming a man." It was like a passage into manhood for me. I received about 30 letters from men, young and old. I still have every one of them in a folder near my bed. I reflect on them periodically and I treasure the insights and concern of these wise men.

One significant letter was written by my Uncle Joe. It was about attitude. The line that stood out the most to me in it was this: "The only thing you have control over is your attitude." Even at 16, I knew there was great wisdom in these words.

There are a lot of hard things that happen in life. Some things we have no control over. Some things we brought upon ourselves. But either way, we can't change them. If we spend time thinking about the past, we inevitably become discouraged or guilt-ridden because, for most of us, there are things that happened in the past that we don't like. Things that happened to us, things we did, or opportunities we missed. Every year that goes by can serve as a reminder of our own imperfection and the corresponding consequences.

We should learn from our past, but not dwell on it.

Similarly, if we think too much of our future, it is likely that we will become anxious or paranoid. "What if a certain scenario plays out? What if I run out of money? What if he leaves? What if they let me down? What if I fail?" Worrying about the future will only make us anxious and distracted.

We should plan for the future, but not obsess over it.

When we regret the past or worry about the future there is one constant result: we miss the present. That's where attitude comes in. We can control where we put our minds. The only place we have to live is in the here and now. Right now...this very moment.

What will you make of this moment? What will you make of **today**?

Regardless of circumstances—past, present, or future—you can control your attitude today. You can control how you live right now. You can determine how you will respond no matter what the world throws at you—no matter how miserably you may fail.

To live this way means taking control of our minds. "Fix your thoughts on what is true and honorable and right. Think about things that are pure and lovely and admirable. Think about things that are excellent and worthy of praise" (Philippians 4:8).

This is does not mean we live in denial of reality. The key is to keep our minds focused on the things that matter most, regardless of what's happening in the world around us. What will you think about today to keep your mind on things that are true?

  "The mind can make heaven of hell, or hell of heaven." – unknown

Write down a worry right here in the space below. Maybe it's regret from the past or fear for the future. Draw a line through it.

_____

_____

_____

Now write down a new attitude that will replace the old.

_____

_____

_____

_____

_____

Imagine in your mind how focusing on this new attitude—new per-spective—will inform your daily mindset and outlook on life. Then walk it out! Every time the old thought or attitude comes back to mind, stop, reject it, refocus, and replace the old thought with your renewed attitude.

_____

_____

_____

_____

_____

_____

_____

_____

_____

_____

_____

It sounds simple, and it actually is. It just takes consistency.

 body
DON'T BE A STATISTIC

35

"Eat to live; don't live to eat." – unknown

A Y staff member tells this story:

> "I met a girl named Megan on the treadmill. She joined the Y about a year ago and has lost 60 pounds by just exercising more and watching what she eats. Her weight loss inspired her mom to join her. Now Megan and her mom meet at the Y three to four mornings a week to exercise together, strengthening their bond with one another as well as their bodies.
>
> Both Megan and her mom, at one point, felt hopelessly overweight and out of shape. But Megan just needed to see progress—and understand that self-discipline works. Megan's mom just needed support."

A story like that is the good news. Unfortunately, Megan and her mom are the exception and not the rule. Here's the tragic reality of our nation's physical health, found in recent U.S. obesity statistics:

1. 58 million overweight, 40 million obese, 3 million morbidly obese
2. Eight out of 10 people over 25 are overweight
3. 78% of Americans are not meeting basic activity level recommendations

These statistics tell us that Megan and her mom are not alone in their struggle with food and exercise. For Americans everywhere, not only has exercise become drudgery, but food has become an indulgence. What a deadly combination! We use food to make us feel better. We eat excessively because we can. We buy it in mass quantities because we can afford to, and it's readily available. Our standard of living has steadily increased, while our (healthy) living standards have plummeted. Many of us are sick.

Here we have a pattern of two extremes: Most Americans dramatically overeat—and under-exercise. We can't seem to find the healthy balance. We over-analyze and under-appreciate our bodies. And we're killing them.

One comment marks an overwhelming number of people who have lost a significant amount of weight, changed their eating habits, and incorporated physical fitness into their regular routine: **"This was the best thing I ever did for myself—I don't know why I didn't do it sooner!"**

If you're going to be a statistic for how you manage your life with regard to food and exercise, be a statistic for healthy change. One day, you'll be saying the same thing: **"Why didn't I do this sooner?"**

 "Strength is the capacity to break a chocolate bar into four pieces with your bare hands—and then just eat one of the pieces." – Judith Viorst

What is one simple, healthy change that you can make immediately regarding your eating habits? _____

_____

_____

_____

Regarding your exercise habits? _____

_____

_____

_____

"Timely silence is precious, for it is nothing less than the mother of the wisest thoughts." – Diadochus of Photiki

According to a recent New York Times article, our minds are suffering from information overload. "Scientists say juggling email, phone calls and other incoming information can change how people think and behave. They say our ability to focus is being undermined by bursts of information."[1]

Bursts of information through any/all of our constantly flowing digital outlets are addictive stimuli. Every few minutes we feel like we have to check our social media of choice, look at our phone, check our email...we're addicted.

"'Technology is rewiring our brains,'" says Nora Volkow, director of the National Institute of Drug Abuse and one of the world's leading brain scientists. She and other researchers compare the lure of digital stimulation less to that of drugs and alcohol than to food and sex, which are essential but counterproductive in excess."[2] With every new hit of real-time information we get a quick little adrenaline rush. With every new notification we get a small energy charge. We're training our minds to continually think of the next "burst" of input. Something new. Something relevant. Something with just enough excitement to hook our brains.

But we're also getting frazzled. More and more of us are having difficulty remaining in the moment or connecting meaningfully with other people.

I was recently watching a sporting event on television with a friend. At the beginning of the game the announcer came over the loud-speaker and informed everyone in the stadium and watching on television that we'd be observing a "moment of silence" in honor of an athlete who'd just tragically died. The stadium went quiet. My living room when quiet. "Thank you," the announcer said to indicate that the time was up. And it was kind of a relief.

We're giving the term "awkward silence" a whole new meaning. Any-time there's silence in the course of our normal day, it's almost awkward. What's missing? What should I be doing? What's on TV? Who's online right now?

Think about how many times in a day you completely disconnect and have a few moments of uninterrupted silence, if it happens at all. How does that go for you? I've asked several people that question this week, and they tell me it's mild torture. They don't know what to do with silence. They're not used to being alone with nothing but themselves, and it's uncomfortable.

Many people go from news in the morning to radio on their commute to constant connectivity through phones and computers throughout the day, and then back to television at night. Distraction has become a lifestyle..

The only moment you have to live in is right now. But what if you're never actually experiencing the here and now? What if distraction is dulling your experience of most moments...and life is simply rushing by without you?

I suggest that silence is the antidote to the frazzled lifestyle. Not just quietness, but quietness that is disconnected from media and anything else distracting. Silence that is reflective, present, aware. A moment of silence—even if it's awkward—just might be the beginning of a new level of health, and a new experience of life.

Similarly, engagement is the antidote to distraction. That means being fully in the moment with whatever we're doing, or with the people around us. Paying attention. Being intentional and focused, not frantically rushing off—either physically or mentally—to the next thing.

It takes discipline to shut off the noise, the activity, and all the stimulation and force our brains to focus on just one thing at a time. But we have to. Our health depends on it.

Question: When is the best time of the day for a few moments of silence? When you first wake up? When you have breakfast? While you drive? _____

_____

_____

_____

_____

Action: Here is a sample exercise you can practice this week.

1. Disconnect from distractions. This might mean going into the closet or car. Perhaps it's going for a walk.
2. Consider your day. Think about everything that happened today or everything that is still to come.
3. Write down details. You'll inevitably think of things you need to do or tasks to accomplish. So write them down and then go back to reflecting.

4. Notice your thoughts. Be aware of the directions in which your mind wants to go. What's the attraction? Perhaps those are the top priorities in your life. Perhaps they are worrisome thoughts and fears. Identify them.
5. Reflect on truth. Draw your mind back to thoughts that are true, helpful, positive, empowering, and beneficial. So much time is wasted on worry. Capture this moment and train your mind to reflect on what's good.

_____

_____

_____

_____

_____

_____

_____

_____

_____

_____

"Brothers and sisters, think about the things that are good and worthy of praise. Think about the things that are true and honorable and right and pure and beautiful and respected...And the God who gives peace will be with you." – Philippians 4:8–9

1. Richtel, Matt, *Attached to Technology and Paying a Price*, New York Times, June 6, 2010.
2. Ibid

spirit
HAPPINESS AND HARMONY

37

"So I decided there is nothing better than to enjoy food and drink and to find satisfaction in work. Then I realized that this pleasure is from the hand of God. For who can eat or enjoy anything apart from him?" – Solomon, Ecclesiastes 2:24-25

Happiness is elusive. But we pursue it all the time. We look for it on TV, in theaters, in bars, and in nightclubs. We chase moments of fleeting happiness in food, alcohol, drugs, sexual encounters, and other temporary thrills and highs. We spend money hoping to acquire happiness in the latest toy or experience.

And underneath it all has developed an increasingly strong vacuum of discontent.

Real happiness, on the other hand, is a joy coming from within us. When our spirits come alive, genuine happiness and contentment are generated from within us...and flow out of us to others. That's what makes some people so contagiously joyful and fun to be around. Those people have probably found God to be their "happy-source."

Jesus said, "Rivers of living water will brim and spill out of the depths of anyone who believes in Me" (John 7:38). God's is a joy without a hangover. And when our spirits begin to receive joy and contentment from God, we will realize that everything good comes from God. "If God gives us wealth and property and lets us enjoy them, we should be grateful and enjoy what we have worked for. It is a gift from God" (Ecclesiastes 5:19).

God loves to give gifts. Yes, we have to work. Yes, we experience disappointment, pain, and betrayal, among other challenges. But amidst all the realities of life, our spirits can rest assured that God is trustworthy.

We can experience real happiness when we're willing trust God for it instead of looking for it in all the wrong places.

 "Tell those who are rich in this world not to be proud and not to trust in their money, which will soon be gone. But their trust should be in the living God, who richly gives us all we need for our enjoyment." – 1 Timothy 6:17

When our spirits are in tune with God's, we can experience happiness and joy regardless of the circumstances. In every season of life, we can agree with those who have proclaimed throughout history: "I will still be joyful and glad, because the Lord God is my Savior" (Habakkuk 3:18).

What has this month done for your total health: body, mind, heart, spirit? What new ideas do you have about health and its connection to our Creator God? _____

_____

_____

_____

What new life-patterns and decisions have you made, or will you make? Which friends and family members will go with you on this lifelong journey toward health and toward God? _____

_____

_____

_____

_____

"May the God of hope fill you with all joy and peace as you trust in him." – Romans 15:13

body
A TIME TO TRAIN

38

"Every man is the builder of a temple called his body." – Henry David Thoreau

Joe is a personal trainer. He helps people reach their fitness goals with encouragement, accountability, and a consistent plan. Recently, one of Joe's clients came to Joe with a problem.

"Joe, it's like I've hit a wall. At first, the thought of getting back into shape was exciting, and when I saw some of the immediate results I was motivated to keep at it. But I've hit a plateau...a dry spot. I'm not seeing new results and I just don't feel like working out anymore—not to mention, my job is really busy and I don't have much energy left at the end of the day."

Joe's response? He identified the operative word in the trainee's complaint: "feel." **I don't FEEL like working out.** Joe pointed out to his client that you can't always depend on your feelings to set your pace and direction. Sometimes you have to set your will and determination to a task and, like the Nike slogan says, **Just do it.**

Feelings are real, and we can't escape them. But we don't have to live our lives being yanked around by them. One key to living a life of health is to realize we have choices as to how we react to these kinds of "feelings." We can behave according to our beliefs, values, and priorities even though our **feelings** may cry out for a different response.

Here are some tips for responding appropriately to feelings:

1. **Identify what the feeling actually is.** All negative feelings are not necessarily simply "anger," "sadness," or "laziness." Those are rather broad categories. Develop your "feeling vocabulary" to help you identify what you are really experiencing. Maybe "anger" is really **jealousy** or **frustration**. Maybe "sadness" is really a sense of **rejection** or **loss**. And maybe that "laziness" you're dealing with is really a **fear of failure** or a **rebellion** against what you know you ought to do. Be honest. It's hard to address something when you don't call it what it is.

2. **Think about things that are true.** What is true in this situation? (e.g. Even though I "feel" like sitting on the couch and watching a movie, I know that exercising right now is better for me in the long run.)

3. **Motivate yourself; don't discourage yourself.** Be your own best cheerleader. Replace any negative self-talk and emotions with thoughts that are true, encouraging, and self-appreciating. Feelings will try to talk you into a different agenda—don't give in! Talk back to yourself and convince yourself of what's true, what's better, and what's healthy.

4. **Hang out with positive, action-oriented people**—the kind of people who are doing what you want to be doing., the kind of people who tell you what you **need** to hear, not what you want to hear.

"There is a time for everything, and a season for every activity under heaven..." – Ecclesiastes 3:1

Life is marked by different seasons. There are seasons of rest, seasons of hard work, seasons of starting, seasons of maintaining, seasons of newness, seasons of faithful repetition, seasons of little, seasons of plenty, seasons of easy, and seasons of effort.

Throughout different seasons—in fact, throughout each day—our feelings change, too. Sometime we enjoy the season we're in. Sometimes we dislike it. Sometimes we feel like pushing ourselves to reach our goals. Sometimes we feel like giving up...or at least putting it off.

There are seasons of life, and you're entering into a new season. For many of us, this is the season of **change**. Just because personal training hasn't been a part of your life before (or lately), doesn't mean you can't start now. Change is a good thing.

mind
LIFELONG LEARNER

39

`Humility = Teachability

Are you teachable? If so, from whom are you learning? I would suggest that you are learning from anyone from whom you are willing to learn.

The wise realize that they can learn something from anyone.

I recently attended a leadership seminar where a former president was interviewed. Because of this president's track record and political positions, there were more than a few people in the room who were grossly turned off by the thought of learning from him. A number of people protested the session, saying, "We are disappointed that this man was included in the leadership event."

In essence, what the protesters were saying was, "We are too prejudiced, proud, and self-righteous to learn anything from this speaker." The protesters who didn't attend the event missed out on a very humble and insightful interview with a good man who has much to offer in the ways of leading people.

I regret my days in school when I sat bored and inattentive in numerous classes. Looking back, I'm sure there was so much more I could've learned had I tried. I'm sure each teacher was a wealth of information in some way, on some subject—had I cared enough to discover the value of his or her experience.

Besides the value of being a lifelong learner, there is also value in considering oneself a "teacher." You, too, have valuable experiences. No one has lived the life you have lived. That makes you more of an expert on your experiences and insights than anyone else. You understand things that I don't. I understand things that you don't. Even someone with no education living in a grass hut on the opposite side of the world could teach us immensely about some aspect of life—if we both cared enough to listen, and to learn.

Here are just a few simple things that help me to be an ongoing learner:

1. Ask a lot of questions
2. Consider each person's uniqueness
3. Seek to learn something every day
4. Ask God for more wisdom

Why is it that sometimes we feel "too stupid" to ask for help? Are we supposed to have it all figured out? Is it really a sign of weakness if we can't understand something? Or might it be weakness if we refuse to ask questions and learn?

Just asking ...

 "If any of you lacks wisdom, he should ask God, who gives generously to all without finding fault, and it will be given to him." – James 1:5

"A wise person is hungry for truth, while the fool feeds on trash." – Proverbs 15:14

Who in your life right now could teach you more than you are allowing him or her to teach you? _____

_____

_____

Is there an area of life you struggle with or want to learn more about?(e.g. technology, time management, cooking, parenting, relationships, financial discipline)? Are you open to learning?

_____
_____
_____
_____
_____
_____

What are some particular things you want to learn about this year? Write down two steps you will take to do it. _____

_____
_____
_____
_____
_____
_____
_____
_____
_____
_____

spirit
CHASE NOTHING

40

"I have learned the secret of being content in any and every situation, whether well fed or hungry, whether living in plenty or in want."
— Apostle Paul, Philippians 4:12

Bill is a good friend of mine. He's one of those friends from the past whom I don't see or talk to often but we still feel close. He is an example to me of a younger man who is experiencing the secret of contentment more than most. And get this, he lives in Newport Beach, CA—the capital of social status and ambition.

Surrounded by money, fancy cars, and living, breathing Barbie dolls, Bill has another kind of secret. He lives with terminal cancer. It's untreatable. Fortunately, it's also slow-moving.

When a doctor tells you at 18 years old that your days are numbered, something happens. That "something" is different for different people. But some kind of change is inevitable. Some might fall into depression and quit on life. Some might travel the world. Others might throw themselves into work and try to make a lot of money as quickly as possible. Others might dive into relationships looking for love, or at least temporary companionship.

Looking at Bill's life 15 years later, it seems he chose a different path. Bill doesn't have enough time in the day to return the phone calls, emails, and messages from of all the people who want to be his friend. His friendship is in such high demand because of the man he's chosen to be.

Since his life on earth is not guaranteed, Bill has a more long-term perspective—that is, eternity. The idea of heaven is one that Bill clings to, and he lives accordingly. He values people over possessions. He is present in each moment. He serves others like it's his job. He writes, performs, and produces music. Everything he does is like a chorus to an already enduring song of legacy.

Now, Bill might live 40 more years—and he might not. Either way, he approaches each day like it might be his last. And as a result, he's one of my favorite human beings to be around.

I don't yet possess the level of peace and perspective in life that my friend Bill has. Neither do I pretend to have "learned the secret" to the degree that Paul describes in the quote above. There are still many days and moments that leave me feeling unsatisfied, restless, or jaded. And I'm careful in my "pursuit" of Paul's level of contentment, as it's not a matter of ambition.

Ambition, you see, is birthed out of restlessness and envy of what others have accomplished. The secret to being content in every situation is something else altogether. It's an inner journey marked by consistent decisions in the midst of difficulty. You can still achieve great things in life and be a person of peace. Or, you can achieve great things in life and remain unfulfilled, unhappy, and unsatisfied.

Reflecting on this truth one day, I wrote in monstrous letters in my journal: CHASE NOTHING. For me, it's a reminder that there's nothing else "out there" that I need. My needs are met. My soul can rest. Every achievement, advancement, or success is pure bonus.

Don't misunderstand me. I have plenty of vision and lots of goals. There are things in me that I want to give or express to the world. But they don't define me. And I'm learning not to wait until some future day to feel like I'm more fully me. I'm me already.

You, too, can be satisfied with you right now, needing nothing more:

- No relationship
- No amount of money
- No fame or recognition
- No retribution or revenge

If you're not satisfied today without it, you won't be satisfied tomorrow with it.

On the journey toward contentment there are no awards or outer signs of arrival. There's no fanfare. No guarantee of social status. No promise of possessions or success. Even if someone writes about you in a book they might change your name to "Bill" and over-simplify your journey.

But there is something that trumps it all: peace.

Question: When have you experienced the strongest sense of peace in your life? What does that tell you?

_____

_____

_____

_____

_____

_____

_____

_____

FINISHING UP

Congratulations on reaching the 40-day goal! And guess what; that was just the introduction.

These last 40 days we've spent together have been an opportunity for you to ingest some thoughts and principles for improving your overall health. I believe that, for all of us, taking time out to pay attention to these ideas is absolutely crucial to our state of well-being.

No matter your age, regardless of your place in life, there is more for you yet to become, more for you yet to do. Continue to give yourself the best chance to reach your God-given potential by committing to your ongoing health and growth—and not just with diet and exercise, but with an awareness of and attentiveness to your whole self.

Throughout this book, you've had the opportunity to replace certain unhealthy thoughts, ideas, and habits with new ones. Whether you've fully taken advantage of this opportunity or not, this is just the beginning. Look back over the notes you made over the past weeks. Consider the actions steps you listed and decide which few are the most important—the ones you will commit to well beyond your experience with this little book.

Every day is a journey. Every day is an opportunity to be YOU, and to be a healthier version of you. It's been said that God is not as interested in your perfection as He is in your direction.

Here's to your lifelong journey toward a healthier YOU!

CALEB ANDERSON is a speaker, writer, consultant, and coach who serves directly with the YMCA of Pierce and Kitsap Counties in Washington State in their Mission and Community Initiatives. Caleb is a graduate of the University of Southern California with a degree in Business Communications. As a result of his own life journey, Caleb is an avid believer in learning to replace personal failure and disappointment with a relentless, faith-filled enthusiasm for life, and has a passion to help the people around him reach the potential for which they were created. When he's not working, he enjoys reading and playing beach volleyball (formerly captain of the USC Men's Volleyball Team and member of the 1998 USA Junior National Volleyball Team). Caleb and his wife, Hilary, live in Gig Harbor, WA .

Stay connected to Caleb for future projects, encouragement, and helpful tools.

http://CalebAnderson.net
Twitter.com/calebanderson
Facebook.com/Chewables.ca